GENDER, DELINQUENCY AND SOCIETY

Gender, Delinquency and Society

A Comparative Study of Male and
Female Offenders and Juvenile
Justice in Britain

DOREEN ELLIOTT
University College, Cardiff

Avebury

Aldershot · Brookfield USA · Hong Kong · Singapore · Sydney

Published by

Avebury

Gower Publishing Company Limited
Gower House
Croft Road
Aldershot
Hants GU11 3HR
England

Gower Publishing Company
Old Post Road
Brookfield
Vermont 05036
USA

British Library Cataloguing in Publication Data

Elliott, Doreen
  Gender, delinquency and society: a comparative study of male and female offenders and juvenile justice in Britain.
  1. Juvenile delinquency—Great Britain—Sex differences
  I. Title
  364.3'6'0941   HV9145.A5

Library of Congress Cataloging-in-Publication Data

Elliott, Doreen.
  Gender, delinquency, and society.

  Bibliography: p.
  Includes index.
  1. Juvenile delinquency—Great Britain—Sex differences—Case studies. 2. Juvenile justice, Administration of—Great Britain—Case studies. 3. Delinquent girls—Great Britain—Case studies.
  I. Title.
  HV9145.A5E45 1988   364.3'6'0941   87–11985

ISBN 0 566 05499 X

Contents

Figures

Tables

Acknowledgements

The author is indebted to the Clerks of the Magistrates' Courts, the Directors of Social Services, the Directors of Education, the Chief Probation Officers and the Chief Constable in the two locations in which the research took place, for their co-operation and agreement to the research taking place within their respective agencies.

Particular thanks are due to the following representatives of those agencies who facilitated the data collection in their departments with unfailing patience and courtesy: Peter Brice, Norman Chapple, Phil Harris, Michael Heap, Linda Kingsberry, Eleri Rees, Barbara Strachan, Christine Walby and W.R. Watkins. Special thanks in this respect go to Sylvia Scarfe; the study benefited greatly from her interest and her experience.

A number of Social Workers and Probation Officers were involved in filling in data sheets on the social background of the young offenders and thanks are due to them for their help in this respect, and also to Marilyn Gardner for the care and patience with which data was collected. Thanks are due also to the Juvenile Liaison Sergeants in each location, who assisted with data collection.

Professor Howard Jones encouraged the early stages of the research and his suggestions were most helpful in furthering the study.

Many thanks go to Sally Barnes for such generous assistance with the computer analysis of the data and statistical advice.

Thanks are extended also to John Howarth, Mike Levi and Ian Shaw, colleagues at University College Cardiff, for their helpful comments at different stages of the project.

Cynthia Diggins and Lindsey Nicholas typed pages of difficult handwriting with customary humour and skill. Ron Walton's interest and encouragement and comments on the final draft, were much appreciated.

Abstract

This study reports research undertaken into gender bias in the juvenile justice system at two levels: the police consultative panels, and the juvenile courts. The research was carried out in two locations, one a major city and the other a nearby small town. Gender comparisons of panel and court decisions were carried out controlling for a number of variables relating to offending patterns such as previous history, type of offence charged, seriousness of offence and age. The section relating to young people appearing before the juvenile court also reports data on a gender comparison of family background and socio-economic status and on location differences between the town and the city.

The theoretical context of the literature on women and crime is reviewed. The research context of gender comparative studies is also reviewed with reference to the incidence and pattern of male and female delinquency, gender comparative studies of the judicial process and studies of gender and social background.

The conclusions emphasize the complexity of the nature of gender bias evident in the present study. Sometimes it operates in favour of females, sometimes against, and clearly refutes the general assumption of many who work in relation to the courts in the role of police officers, court officials, probation officers and social workers, that a 'chivalrous' approach to females influences the judicial process.

1 Women, girls, crime and delinquency: the theoretical context

Few, if any, other traits have as great statistical importance as does sex in differentiating criminals from non-criminals. (Sutherland and Cressey, 1960, p.114)

Official statistics indicate that of all those found guilty or cautioned for indictable offences in England and Wales, females account for 17 per cent of the total (HMSO, 1981, p.83). In the USA females constitute 19.5 per cent of all persons arrested. The ratio of male to female arrests for violent crime was 8 : 1, and for property crime 3.5 : 1 (FBI, 1980).

The figures for juveniles alone are very similar. Females under 16 make up approximately 19 per cent of all juvenile offenders (DHSS, 1981), and in the USA females under 18 constitute 22 per cent of all offenders under 18 (FBI, 1980).

This difference in the male and female crime rate also holds good for an examination of cross-cultural statistics. Simon and Sharma (1979) quote data collected by the International Police Organization for twenty-five countries from 1963 to 1972. The average percentage of females among all arrests during that decade is consistently low: the highest percentages were for the West Indies, where women accounted for 20.9 per cent of all crime committed, and New Zealand (20.56 per cent), with Hong Kong (2.76 per cent), Fiji (2.67 per cent) and Brunei (2.02 per cent) being the lowest. Figures for England and Wales at that time were 13.61 per cent, and for Scotland 11.53 per cent and the USA 13.66 per cent. Thus this cross-cultural comparison of arrests shows that, at the highest, little more than one-fifth of women were arrested and the mean for the twenty-five countries was 11.1 per cent.

Despite the fact that the quotation above from Sutherland and Cressey appeared in the first edition of their classic work, in 1923, most research studies or reviews of the literature on female offenders begin by acknowledging the dearth of work on women criminals and delinquents in comparison with that on the male offender:

> The criminality of women is a neglected field of research ... female criminality deserves more research interest than it has received, no matter how small its numerical importance may appear on the basis of criminal statistics taken at their face value. (Pollak, 1961, p.xv)

> First of all, we do not even begin to have a 'natural history' of female deviance, our knowledge of its parameters, its structure and sub-structures, the types and nature of activities which make it up, are all exceedingly limited. (Heidensohn, 1968)

> The criminality of women has long been a neglected subject area of criminology ... Female criminality has often ended up as a footnote to works on men that purport to be works on criminality in general. (Klein, 1973, p.3)

> Our knowledge of the nature of female criminality is still in its infancy. In comparison with the massive documentation on all aspects of male delinquency and criminality, the amount of work carried out in the area of women and crime is extremely limited. (Smart, 1977, p.1)

> The crime and delinquency committed by women and girls in American society has commanded little interest from those institutions and agencies that have traditionally devoted a great deal of attention to male delinquency. (Datesman and Scarpitti, 1980, p.3)

The application of criminological theory to female offenders

It is certainly true that most theoretical formulations about the aetiology, nature and extent of crime and delinquency refer to male criminal behaviour. Until recently no systematic attempt had been made to apply theories such as anomie, differential association, labelling, sub-cultural theory and a radical criminology perspective to the criminal behaviour of females. Leonard (1982) provides a summary, a general critique and a feminist critique to each group of theories. Campbell (1981) discusses the theories and their application to females in more general terms, and Box (1983) suggests that these theories have a valid contribution to make to the understanding of female crime.

Anomie

Merton's (1938) theory of anomie and crime distinguishes between goals which are socially learned and culturally determined and the means available to achieve these goals. Merton associated these goals with financial success. Leonard (1982) argues that Merton's theory can be applied to women and crime only by revising our understanding of what the goals which are culturally determined might be for women. She argues that financial success is not a goal which is important in Western society for most women, who are socially conditioned to achieve their primary fulfilment through marriage and children. Morris (1964) argues similarly that for females the most important social goals are to negotiate successful affective relationships. Both Morris and Leonard suggest that in these terms their culturally determined goals are more easily achieved by women than by men, and that this might go some way towards explaining the sex difference in the crime rate. Leonard goes on to argue that this explanation is not entirely satisfactory, however, since it does not explain the female crime which does exist, such as prostitution and shoplifting, and that women do not fit easily into Merton's categories of response (i.e. conformity, innovation, ritualism, retreatism and rebellion). Is a middle-aged, middle-class shoplifter a conformist or a rebel? Leonard fails to add the criticism also that self-report studies of female crime show less difference between the sexes, both in the nature and in the extent of female crime, than official statistics indicate, and this inevitably weakens the case that even a revised Merton's anomie theory explains female crime.

Support . Murton

Criticism

Differential association

Sutherland and Cressey's (1960) theory of differential association was based on the assumption that criminal behaviour is learned, mainly in primary reference groups, and that a person becomes delinquent when they have more exposure to codes and patterns of behaviour which are deviant than to those which are conformist.

Leonard (1982), in applying the theory of differential association to women, argues that the idea that crime is learned from primary reference groups helps to explain the lower rate of female crime and delinquency. She suggests that females are more closely supervised by their families and that the family remains a more important refer-

3

ence group for adolescent females than it does for adolescent males. However, she also puts forward the critique that given that males and females share the same neighbourhoods and families, then differential association does not satisfactorily explain why their behaviour pattern appears to be so very different. The degree of determinism implicit within differential association is also problematic. Leonard argues that subsequent to the Second World War when many rigid norms were broken down, the role of women has become increasingly less passive. Perhaps the greatest advantage, argues Leonard, of Sutherland's theory in its application to women is that in emphasizing that criminal behaviour is learned it moves away from the idea of biological determinism, which as will be seen later, has been a dominant influence in the literature on female crime. Sutherland's theory also reinforces the notion that women and men are treated unequally in our society and that males and females from the same families and reference groups in fact have very different experiences.

Sub-cultural theory

Cohen (1955), Miller (1958) and Cloward and Ohlin (1960) are major contributors to the sub-cultural school of criminological theory. Cohen argues that in male working-class groups the existence of status discontent leads to formation of sub-cultural groups which violate and oppose middle-class norms. Miller denies that the gang is a reaction to middle-class norms and emphasizes that it has its own validity within working-class culture in expressing and characterizing the issues of trouble, toughness, smartness, excitement, fate and autonomy. Cloward and Ohlin draw on Merton's and Sutherland's ideas in proposing that working-class males develop three kinds of sub-culture: a criminal sub-culture, a conflict sub-culture, characterized by hooliganism and violence, and a retreatist sub-culture, characterized by 'dropping out' and by the use of drugs. A major criticism of this school of thought is that if it were valid there would be more working-class crime than there is, since not all working-class males are criminal, and that it does not take account of the fact that criminal behaviour occurs which is not confined to the working-class. Its application is limited to urban, working-class, male delinquency.

Leonard argues that it is difficult to apply sub-cultural theories to females, since there exists very little empirical research on female sub-cultures, and that they concentrate on the class variable at the expense of the sex variable. Cohen's view of female sexual delinquency as a response to failure in achieving female norms, that is, successful marital status, fails to explain female property crime and would imply a greater volume of female crime than exists, given our knowledge about unhappiness in families. It also fails to account for the sexualization of female crime as a response of the system. This is, however, more adequately explained by labelling theory.

Labelling theory

This school of thought dominated by Lemert (1951), Becker (1963) and Kitsuse (1962), and associated also with Cicourel (1968) and Schur (1971) amongst others, emphasizes that crime and deviance are socially defined. Because this is so, certain groups having less power or status will be all the more likely to be labelled. It emphasizes the effect that the official process of the law has on the individual's response and thus concentrates on the formation of 'secondary' deviance. A major criticism of this school of thought is that it fails adequately to explore and explain primary deviance.

Leonard (1982) contends that although no systematic analysis of labelling theory has been undertaken with regard to female crime, it nevertheless offers a valuable perspective. It allows recognition of the view that women's role in society is culturally defined and that laws are socially defined by powerful male-dominated interests. It also emphasizes, Leonard argues, the impact of social reaction on individual development: to be labelled obedient, passive and non-violent is a powerful influence on the self-image of women. Although labelling theory is perhaps less fully worked out and more diffuse than other theories, it has nevertheless the most significant contribution to make to an understanding of female crime of any of the major criminological theories.

Radical criminology

The 'new', 'radical' or 'critical' criminology theorists as given expression in the work of Taylor, Walton and Young (1973, 1975), Quinney (1973), Gordon (1973) and Spitzer (1975) largely ignore female crime just as the liberal theorists before them. In the sense that aspects of the new criminology consider oppression — albeit focused on class and race at the expense of sex — and challenge traditional assumptions in criminology, examining the basis for the definition of crime, then it has a contribution to make to the understanding of female criminal and delinquent behaviour. Klein and Kress (1976) argue that radical criminology has made a contribution to the study of female crime. They suggest that it has contributed to the re-definition of rape (as a crime against woman, rather than against a woman who is the property of another man); to the re-interpretation of prostitution focusing on the economic aspects and calling for de-criminalization; and that it has led to a consideration of the issue of mental illness and women, seeing admission to psychiatric hospital as a form of incarceration of large numbers of women. It could be argued, however, that the initiative for these changes has come more from pressure groups than from theorists. Klein and Kress argue that one must not look to traditional criminology for an understanding of women and crime, but to the emerging movements of radical criminology and feminism (1976, p.36).

Female crime

This lack of any serious analysis of female crime by the major schools of criminological theory emphasizes the neglect of the topic. Those studies which have focused specifically on female crime have done so from perspectives about the nature of women that have rightly elicited strong criticism from recent feminist sources (e.g. Smart, 1977; Klein, 1973; Pollak, 1978; Hoffman Bustamante, 1973).

The work of Lombroso and Ferraro (1895) on the female offender, with its emphasis on certain physical characteristics and atavism, which were supposed to predispose an individual to crime, would seem to most people to contain ideas which do not justify serious consideration from our perspective in the latter end of the twentieth century. Yet it is a chastening experience to see how this biological view is consistently reflected in much later works, and how this approach has remained the dominant one at the expense of a proper examination of the sociological and economic aspects of female crime.

The Gluecks (1934) investigated a range of physical and social variables of the 500 females in their study. The sexual history of offenders was included whether or not their offence was related to sexual behaviour. Few, if any, studies of male criminals who are not sex offenders include this kind of material. The Gluecks conclude that criminality was likely to be passed on to the children of offenders, and they even recommended a sterilization programme.

Pollok (1961), like the Gluecks, included a social dimension in his analysis, but like the Gluecks also his conclusions contain a strong biological flavour. Pollak put forward the view that official statistics do not represent the true amount of female crime and that female offending is masked partly by the social role of women, offences committed within the family being less often reported. It is also masked because of the chivalrous reaction of men (i.e. policemen and lawyers) who operate the system and because deceit is built into the very nature of women, argues Pollok. He justifies this view with reference to the fact that women conceal menstruation, and that in sexual intercourse the male cannot conceal his failure to achieve an erection, yet the female can much more easily feign orgasm (ibid., p.10). He sees the passive role of woman as culturally determined (ibid., p.3) and concludes that they more frequently act as instigators in crime, and as such are more difficult to detect. Pollak's biological perspective is clearly displayed in this quotation from his summary chapter:

> The correlation between the incidence of female crime and the period of child bearing age indicated from the start that the biological phenomena which characterise this age period in women deserve our attention. Actually, from this angle, menstruation, pregnancy and menopause have to be considered of central research interest in this respect. (ibid., p.157)

That male criminal careers cover approximately the same age span is rather difficult to account for from Pollak's point of view and highlights the unsatisfactory nature of this perspective.

Female delinquency

This biological perspective is also reflected in views of female delinquency: that female delinquency is perceived as different from, and worse than, male delinquency is clear from these quotations:

> We must never lose sight of the fact ... that female sexual delinquency is far more profoundly self-destructive and irreversible in its corrosive consequences than is male delinquency. (Blos, 1969, p.109)

> There is abundant tragic evidence that sexual delinquency is far more profoundly self-destructive and irreversible in its consequences for a girl than is the delinquency that is seen in boys. (Friedman, 1969, p.113)

> The results of our investigation support the very wide consensus that girl delinquents deviate from sociological and psychological norms much more than boy delinquents ... Pathological psychiatric deviations are much more common in delinquent girls than boys ... Delinquent girls are more often oversized, lumpish, uncouth and graceless, with a raised incidence of minor physical defects. (Cowie, Cowie and Slater, 1968, p.166)

Cowie, Cowie and Slater do not use the concept of atavism (reversion to a lower and more primitive type), as did Lombroso and Ferraro (1895), but nevertheless the parallel is striking across a period of more than seventy years. That seventy years in other fields has covered major technological developments in electronics, space travel and attitudes, yet what an unfortunate comment is implied on the state of criminological theory with regard to females that this parallel is so evident.

Other studies of female offenders emphasize psychiatric disturbance. Felice and Offord (1972) in the conclusion to their study of the characteristics of delinquent girls suggest that future studies would gain from classifying girls under three headings, one of which would be 'psychiatric delinquency'. The view of the female offender as 'disturbed' rather than delinquent has practice implications too: in South Wales there is an institution known as a treatment centre for delinquent girls. Yet comparable institutions in the region for boys are known as community homes or schools. Felice and Offord (1971) in their review of the literature suggest that female delinquency is often seen as a personality disturbance that results in conflict with society, and expressed as a form of sexual deviancy, which Blos claims 'is dynamically close to perversion, a fact which strongly differentiates female delinquency from male delinquency' (ibid., p.22). These are strong terms in which to describe female delinquency and are questionable in the light of recent studies (e.g. Chesney-Lind, 1974) which have drawn attention to the sexualization of female crime by official agencies. (This latter and other studies are discussed more fully in Chapter 2.) Much more down to earth is the viewpoint of the practitioner—researcher Richardson (1969, p.220), who despite the traditional sexist connotations of the use of the adjective 'nice', denies the pathological view: 'There were also many "nice" girls, to whom the sexual part of an arrangement was (if existent) secondary to the material comforts, companionship and the sense of being needed, but one does not have to go to Approved School files only for these stories.'

Konopka (1966) in her study of institutionalized girls emphasizes the emotional origin of the girls' situation: 'What I found in the girl in despair was ... loneliness accompanied by despair ... Adolescent boys, too, often feel lonely and search for understanding and friends. Yet, in general, this does not seem to be the centre core of their problems, not their most outspoken ache' (ibid., p.40), and also reinforces the sexualization of female delinquency:

> Almost invariably, her problems are deeply personalised. Whatever her offense — whether shoplifting, truancy or running away from home — it is usually accompanied by some disturbance or unfavourable behaviour in the sexual area thus involving her own total being and affecting her relationship with others. (ibid., p.4)

Konopka does, however, make reference to some social and cultural issues, including the existence and resentment of the double standard operated for males and females and differential employment opportunities (ibid., p.121). Yet her focus remains strongly psychological and she fails to incorporate these into her undoubtedly sympathetic and well-intentioned account of female delinquency.

Vedder and Somerville, in their study published as recently as 1970, offer a typology of female delinquency as follows: the runaway girl; the incorrigible girl; the sex-delinquent girl; the probation-violated girl; and the truant girl. These types are explained in purely psychological terms: the sex-delinquent girl looking for acceptance and love; the probation-violated girl unable to maintain relationships; the runaway girl using the immature defence of avoidance; and the truant being similar to the runaway but having insufficient independence to make the complete break. Their token recognition of social issues appears in their conclusion where they acknowledge that as the 'social roles of boys and girls become more alike, their delinquent activities [will become] less distinguishable from one another' (1970, p.164).

Trèse (1962) in a study of institutionalized female delinquents again focuses on an interpretation of delinquent behaviour which draws heavily on a psychodynamic psychology. Thomas (1923) also takes a strong psychological approach but the emphasis on the value of rehabilitation and prevention has a strong flavour of paternalistic social control. Davies (1976) in her study of girls appearing before a London juvenile court concludes: 'Two important factors appeared to be prominent in the characteristics of the court girls; first the *disturbed mental state* of certain girls and secondly the incidence of truancy and/or unstable employment' [my italics] (ibid., p.63).

The implications of this strong emphasis on pathology is that the response tends to be on a medical model. Both male and female juveniles have been increasingly subjected to this approach in Britain since the implementation of the Children and Young Persons Act 1969 whose welfare orientation has led inadvertently to a trend to more punitive sentencing of young people. Chapter 2 discusses in more detail how the welfare approach applied to females has led to harsher treatment, and in the USA (in some states) the use of indeterminate sentences for women is justified on 'treatment' lines.

The influence of feminist thought

More recently, from the 1970s onwards, there has emerged a genre in the literature relating to female crime and delinquency which has challenged the views outlined above that had become so entrenched. The influence of the Women's movement is clear.

Anderson (1976) examines the 'chivalrous' treatment of women offenders in the criminal justice system. She finds on reviewing the literature that there is widespread acceptance of the fact that women are treated more leniently than men at all stages of the process: they are less likely to be reported, arrested or be found guilty. Largely because it is mostly men who operate the system and because they are protective towards women, then they are more reluctant to act in the case of female offenders. Anderson asserts that there is little empirical evidence for such a view. Indeed, as Hoffman Bustamante (1973) demonstrates, there is growing evidence some of which is reviewed in Chapter 2 to suggest that for some offences, and at some stages in the judicial process, women are in fact more harshly treated than men.

The Women's movement has generally drawn attention to the gender roles of women in society, emphasizing that whilst sex may be biologically determined, gender is a social and cultural concept and as such is relative, not absolute. The female role in Western society is essentially passive, non-aggressive, sensitive and supportive. Women, therefore, tend to be less involved in offences such as robbery and burglary and would have less access to the skills required to start a motor vehicle without an ignition key, for instance. Hoffman Bustamante argues that when the moralistic assumptions of the traditional studies of women offenders are replaced by a sociological examination of the nature of female crime, then crimes committed by women are the outcome of five major factors:

> These include differential role expectations for men and women, sex differences and socialisation patterns and application of social control, structurally determined differences in opportunities to commit particular offences, differential access or pressure toward criminally oriented sub-cultures and careers and sex differences built into the crime categories themselves. (ibid., p.117)

All of these factors are related to gender role. Shover and Norland (1978) in their examination of sex roles and criminality suggest that amongst other factors 'post factum analysis of research findings' has reinforced 'conventional wisdom' at the expense of scientific knowledge. An example of such biased interpretation of research results can be seen in the conclusion drawn by Mannarino and Marsh (1978) in their examination of the relationship between sex-role identification and juvenile delinquency in girls. They studied a group of sex delinquents, a group of anti-social offenders and a control group for sex-role identity. Their clearest finding was that the anti-social group scored high on masculine traits, but that there was no statistical significance between the sex delinquent group and the control group.

Despite this, they insist that both groups of deviant girls developed 'deviant conscious sex roles' (ibid., p.648).

The issue of gender role and its influence on female crime has led to the debate about the 'New Female Criminal'. Simon (1975) identified a significant increase in the proportion of women involved in crime, and particularly in certain offences such as theft, forgery, fraud and embezzlement, but not in crimes of violence, prostitution or child abuse. She saw this increase as congruent with opportunity theory and the changing role of women resulting from the influence of the Women's movement. Adler's (1975) analysis sees changes in the role of women as a social revolution, which begets a new breed of female criminal who with new-found assertiveness participates in crimes traditionally seen as masculine.

Oakley (1972) argued a strong association between criminality and the characteristics ascribed to the male gender role. Therefore, as the female role takes on more of the attributes traditionally regarded as male attributes, then so female crime increases.

However, others have questioned this direct and linear comparison of the increase in women's crime and the Women's movement. Smith and Visher (1980) analysed forty-four studies which reported on the relationship between sex and criminality. They found it to be dependent on a number of variables such as the year in which the data were collected, the population group from which samples were drawn, the type of offence and whether single or composite indicators of offending were used. Steffensmeir's (1980) analysis of official statistics suggests that any change is due less to change in female crime patterns than to other factors including changes in reporting and law enforcement procedures. Weis (1976) suggests the theory that women's liberation is related to an increase in female crime relies over much on official crime statistics and questions the interpretation of the causal link between 'liberation' and crime. He suggests that most statistics and file reports show that women are not more violent and that the increase in property offences might just as well be accounted for by a depressed economy and widespread unemployment. He argues too that no empirical data exist which show that 'liberated' women are more criminal than those who are not. Smart (1979) suggests that the direct causal link is too simplistic and that the opportunity theory argument does not hold since the Women's movement is not significantly involved in enhancing work opportunities. She, like Weis, argues that other societal changes are taking place which need to be taken into account.

The debate has stimulated work on the female offender and new works have appeared taking a more sociological approach to the study of female crime (Crites, 1976; Bowker, 1978; Adler and Simon, 1979; Datesman and Scarpitti, 1980; Chapman, 1980). Campbell's (1981) study of girl delinquents is an important contribution to the 'new' literature on female crime. She also questions the causal relationship between the Women's movement and female crime patterns, and emphasizes the economic link. Social pressures associated with shoplifting are examined, as are girls' attitudes to violence and aggression.

These developments in the literature are an encouraging change from biological determinism and the individual pathological view of the female offender. However, factors other than the feminist critique have been responsible for challenging traditional views of female offending. Chapter 2 reviews gender comparative studies in assessing the validity of this challenge.

2 Gender and juvenile delinquency: the research context

There is a growing body of evidence from studies comparing male and female offenders which challenges the traditional picture of female delinquency presented by criminologists and others, which was outlined in Chapter 1. This chapter examines the evidence for the challenge to this traditional view by drawing on comparative studies of male and female offenders in three areas: self-report studies concerned with the incidence and pattern of delinquency; comparative studies of process and gender bias in the juvenile justice system; and studies of social background.

I Gender comparative self-report studies: incidence and pattern of male and female delinquency

The existence of an increasing number of self-report studies comparing samples of male and female juvenile delinquents challenges the traditional view of both the *incidence* and *pattern* of female delinquency and also its incidence as represented by official statistics.

The value of self-report studies as a method of research has been disputed on a number of grounds. It is suggested that it is difficult to make a proper comparison of these studies because of differences in sample size, selection and composition, in the type of delinquent acts surveyed, in the wording of items and in research techniques. Bowker's (1978) critique suggests that the problems are threefold: to do with sampling, communication and honesty. Most studies involve limited local rather than national samples; use easily accessible sample groups, such as institutional populations; and represent less powerful groups, for example, juveniles are more frequently used than adults, public schools (USA) rather than élite private schools. With regard to communication, Bowker suggests that individuals may differ substantially in their interpretation of the meaning of questions and that interviewers may consciously or unconsciously communicate their own biases. Honesty may be a problem, in that some respondents may like to project certain images, even to themselves, thus resulting in under- or over-reporting of certain behaviours. Hood and Sparks (1970) in their review of the validity of self-report techniques suggest that an interviewer who attempts to gain rapport by a sympathetic approach may produce concealment on embarrassing items, whilst a cold and authoritarian approach may engender lack of trust.

Nettler (1978) is critical of the self-report study as a research method on the grounds of reliability, validity and research design. Farrington's (1973) study is quoted to illustrate some of the problems: it involved a sample of lower-class urban English boys tested at 14 and 15 years and repeated two years later at 16 and 17 years. The reliability of the first study was assessed by the consistency with the second reports. Farrington found that a quarter of earlier admissions changed into later denials, and that of the more serious crimes half of these were later repudiated. With regard to the validity of self-report studies, Nettler argues that it is unsatisfactory to validate self-report studies with self-report studies and concludes that 'there are good reasons for listening sceptically to what people tell us they have done' (1978, p.113). Research design criticisms include problems associated with interviewing and questionnaires — the instruments used for self-report studies — as well as the problem that the offences selected are weighted heavily to trivial offences. This is borne out by an examination of the questionnaires and interview schedules; Hindelang (1971a) includes cheating in examinations. West and Farrington (1973), Campbell (1976) and Jamison (1977) include an item: 'I have trespassed somewhere I was not supposed to go, like empty houses, railway lines or private gardens'. Short and Nye (1958) and Kratcoski and Kratcoski (1975) include 'defied parents' authority', thus making similarity between the sexes appear greater than it is. Inevitably inclusion of such items might make the similarity between the sexes appear greater than if more serious items only were included. Kratcoski and Kratcoski's study (1975) also included fist fighting, gambling and destroying property and these items showed significant differences between the sexes.

Some of these criticisms are more valid than others. Technical problems associated with the methodology of the research can be allowed for: for example, honesty checks can be included in the questionnaires and interview schedule. Clark and Taft (1966) used a polygraph (lie detector) and a further interview to check the written responses in their study.

A number of self-report studies have shown high correlation between an individual's report of his own delinquency and his official police record (Campbell, 1981, p.15). Campbell in her study took account of the criticism that the inclusion of trivial misdemeanours in the list of items might bias the results by analysing the results for indictable offences only. The results still showed a high correlation between the offences admitted by the male and female samples. There is evidence showing that results of self-report studies do not differ significantly with the variations of method used, for instance, interview or questionnaire, anonymous or otherwise. Hardt and Peterson-Hardt (1977) in a study designed to test the effectiveness of the self-report method found that criticisms of this approach were not substantiated, there being a high degree of validity in the responses to their questionnaire. Gibbons, Morrison and West (1970) also acknowledge albeit more cautiously the validity of the method, having found a 'good correspondence' between admitted crimes and recorded crimes in their sample of known offenders.

The remarkable consistency of results in the following studies, despite the variety of samples and geographical locations, indicates the strength rather than the weakness of the self-report method. The ratios shown in Table 2.1 are much closer to one another than they are to the ratios from official statistics. Overall, although self-report studies may have certain limitations, they are likely to be a more reliable indicator of the extent and nature of juvenile crime than are official statistics with all their attendant problems of classification of data, bias operating at various levels of the system from police on the beat to the decision to charge and problems of accuracy in recording. Official statistics may tell us as much about the system as they do about juvenile delinquency.

The accumulated evidence of the comparative self-report studies summarized below is impressive. They cover a variety of geographical locations mostly in the USA; a range of social class, racial groups and age-groups are represented, covering a period of twenty-one years. Datesman and Scarpitti (1980) neatly summarize the findings of self-report studies as follows:

1   For three decades they have indicated that a great deal of 'hidden' female delinquency exists.
2   Whilst the male and female ratio of the incidence of delinquent behaviour is closer than official statistics suggest, males are how-

ever more involved in delinquent activity than females.
3 The pattern of delinquent behaviour is very similar for both sexes; girls are involved in the same offences but at a different rate.
4 Official statistics greatly exaggerate the sexual nature of female delinquency.

Perhaps, as Farrington (1973) suggests, the most accurate measure of deviant behaviour may yet prove to be some combination of improved official statistics and self-report data.

Self-report studies and the incidence of female delinquency

A number of self-report studies give a ratio figure indicating the overall comparison of male to female admissions to the items in their survey. Some studies (e.g. Clark and Haurek, 1966) give a range of ratios for different offences: 2.31 to 1 overall ratio and 3.7 to 1 for chronic offences, whilst the ratio for major theft was 1.4 to 1. Those studies which indicate an overall ratio have been summarized in Table 2.1. It can be seen that the variation is from 1.33 to 1 (Campbell, 1981), indicating the smallest difference in the overall ratio of male to female offences admitted, with 3.0 to 1 (Feyerhem, 1981) representing the largest difference. Even this largest difference shown up by self-report studies is lower than the ratio calculated from official statistics.

The ratios from official statistics in the USA for the years covering the self-report studies in Table 2.1 vary depending on the date. In 1955 Short and Nye (1958) quote a male–female ratio of 5 to 1 according to Children's Bureau statistics. Other figures show slight variations: 1963, 4 to 1 (Reckless, 1967); 1975, 3.7 to 1 overall ratio for all crimes, with 8.39 to 1 for violent crimes and 4.05 to 1 for property offences (Cernkovitch and Giordano, 1979, using the *FBI Uniform Crime Reports*). In 1979 the overall ratio was 3.8 to 1 (calculated from *FBI Uniform Crime Reports*, 1979, table 31).

Figures for England and Wales over a similar period are set out in Table 2.2. The closing of the gap in the male–female ratio illustrates the trend shown in official statistics to an increase in the amount of female crime recorded and referred to in Chapter 1. Overall these studies confirm the view that much female delinquency remains unrecorded in official statistics.

Not all comparative self-report studies calculate a ratio for incidence of delinquent behaviour and so are not included in the summary Table 2.1. The following section summarizes the major studies carried out after Short and Nye (1958) published their pioneering work. Many of the subsequent studies used some or all of the items on Short and Nye's questionnaire.

Table 2.1 Summary table of comparative self-report studies giving ratios for the incidence of male and female delinquency

Date of research	Author	Date of publication	Number in sample	Nature of sample	Mean overall ratio of male–female offences
1964	Wise	1967	589	Middle class, USA	1.7 to 1
1964–5	Jensen and Eve	1976	4000	Stratified random sample, black and non-black; grades 7–12 high school; USA	No overall ratio quoted; found a range of 1.6 to 1 for 'fighting' in black sub-sample to 6 to 1 for 'grand theft' among both blacks and whites
1966	Clark and Haurek	1966	1116	Urban, rural and industrial communities; mixed class; USA	2.31 to 1
1968	Hindelang	1969	763	Students from Catholic high school in California, USA	2.56 to 1
1973	Weis	1976	555	8th and 11th grade US high schools; middle class	1.95 to 1 (8th grade) 3.15 to 1 (11th grade)
Not reported	Kratcoski and Kratcoski	1975	248	11th and 12th grade, mixed social class; USA	2.0 to 1
1976	Campbell	1981	66 girls compared with 397 boys in West and Farrington's (1973) sample	Working class, British	1.33 to 1
1977	Cernkovich and Giordano	1979	822	Mixed class, 16–18 years; USA	2.18 to 1
1975	Johnson	1979	734	Grades 9–12 in three Seattle high schools, USA	1.5 to 1
1980	Figueira *et al.*	1981	1735	10th grade in three parochial and six public schools, USA	3.6 to 1 (calculated from table 2.1)
Not reported	Feyerhem	1981	1119	Mainly white, working and lower middle class, USA	3.0 to 1

Table 2.2   Ratios of incidence of male and female delinquency in England and Wales, 1965–83

Date	Age	
	10–14	14–17
1965	7.3 to 1	7.1 to 1
1970	6.2 to 1	7.0 to 1
1975	4.1 to 1	5.4 to 1
1978	3.6 to 1	5.0 to 1
1983	3.2 to 1	4.8 to 1

Source: Home Office, *Criminal Statistics (England and Wales)*, 1983, Table 5.18.

Self-report studies and the pattern of female delinquency

It was the work of Short and Nye (1958) which pioneered the self-report study and inspired many later studies. Their research compared boys' and girls' responses to their questionnaire administered to high school groups in two locations and to an institutionalized (training school) group. Their findings indicate some similarities and some differences with official statistics. Their study found that boys commit virtually all offences more frequently than girls, but that the ratio of 5 : 1 was not borne out by their research, suggesting a bias towards under-reporting female delinquency in the official figures. Short and Nye found similarities in their self-report data, with the exception of female status offences. Status offences were found to be not significantly different in the male and female sub-samples, and they conclude 'the fact that girls are most often referred to court for such activities presumably reflects society's greater concern for the unsupervised activities of girls' (ibid., p.57).

Clark and Haurek (1966) investigated the relationship between age and sex attributes and misconduct from an interactionist view of delinquency. They found that where official statistics put the male–female ratio for the incidence of delinquency at 5 : 1 or 4 : 1, in their study they found that out of thirty-six items on their questionnaire, on only four offences did the ratio exceed 4 : 1. They comment that this is more striking when the absence of sex offences from their data is considered. They conclude that official statistics considerably exaggerate the greater male propensity for occasional misconduct and suggest that the general view of the female sex role is a factor in the gender bias in the system.

The findings of Short and Nye (1958) were confirmed by Clark (1967), whose 1961 study of 200 female and 462 male institutionalized juveniles showed an even greater similarity between females and males in the pattern of self-reported crime than she had expected. Clark concluded that the pattern of female crime, that is, type of offences committed, approximated to that of male delinquents. This study also showed similarity between the male and female samples in respect of age and friends with whom offences were committed. This represented a discrepancy with the recorded pattern which showed that 74 per cent of the female sample had been committed for status offences.

Wise (1967) used for her study the null hypothesis that 'among middle-class adolescents girls will not differ significantly from boys in either the volume or the type of their reported delinquent behaviour' (p.182). Whilst differences were reported in the amount of delinquent behaviour in the male and female group, these two groups reported participating about equally in alcohol and sex-related offences.

A much later study by Weis also used a middle-class sample, and his findings are in line with those of Wise (1967) as well as with other studies, in that he concluded: 'There are significant sex differences in the prevalence, incidence and seriousness of delinquent involvement' but also that 'the *patterns* of delinquent involvement by sex and age are similar' (1975, p.23). However, he found that girls were less violent than boys.

Work carried out by Gold has made an important contribution to research in this field of comparative self-report studies. Gold's (1970) survey based on a sample of 522 adolescents in Michigan showed differences in the incidence of delinquency in the male and female sub-samples, but concluded that the pattern of delinquency is similar. He found that status offences accounted for only 8 per cent of the offences admitted by the girls and only 6 per cent of offences admitted by the boys in the study, highlighting once again the differences in the pattern between official records and admitted delinquency.

Gold and his colleagues also carried out two national surveys of youth which aimed to focus on the nature and frequency of juvenile offending in the USA. Williams and Gold (1972) in their report of the first survey undertaken in 1967 indicate that boys are more delinquent than girls, but aside from the more serious property and aggressive crimes distribution was more similar between the sexes than is usually recognized. Status offences were shown to represent only 11 per cent of the girls' delinquencies. The second national survey of youth carried out five years later and reported by Gold and Reiman (1975) indicated that the differences between male and female offending had reversed: boys reported less delinquency than in the first survey, girls reported more delinquency.

Jensen and Eve (1976) re-examined the data from a survey undertaken in 1964—5 by the Survey Research Centre, University of California. The data were gathered from 4000 adolescents in Richmond, California. The data in this survey had been extensively analysed by Hirschi (1969) in relation to the males, and Jensen and Eve used the data with the intention of comparing the male and female groups. The data included only criminal offences and excluded status offences, and therefore are rather different in character to that in other studies which included both. However, it is interesting to note that 'the most common of the six offences among the Richmond females closely parallels the pattern for Richmond males' (Jensen and Eve, 1976, p.435). The difference in the pattern of male and female offending was found to be statistically significant — but weak. They attributed some of this difference to the fact that numbered questionnaires were administered by teachers in classrooms, and they felt that females would be less willing than males to admit delinquent acts. They take their analysis further by introducing a number of variables to explain the sex difference, such as relationships with parents, attitudes to conventional moral norms, youth culture and friendship patterns, but without strongly conclusive results.

Hindelang (1971a) concluded from his study of 319 males and 474 females in a Catholic high school, in California, that:

> The pattern of female delinquent involvement, although at a reduced frequency, parallels quite closely the pattern of male delinquency; when the mean frequencies of delinquent involvement are ranked for both the males and the females, the rank-order correlation coefficient is found to be .925 (p<001), which indicates that the most and least frequent activities among the males and females are nearly identical. This finding is at odds with the conception of female delinquents as engaging primarily in 'sex' delinquencies. (ibid., p.533)

Walberg and Yeh (1974) in their study of 196 boys and 234 girls in three Chicago high schools concentrate on family background and ethnicity as well as sex in relation to delinquency. Their findings confirm the view that boys report more delinquency and are more often involved in serious delinquency and that certain gender differences operate in the pattern of delinquency: for example, white boys are more often involved in car thefts and black girls more often report involvement in gang fights.

Kratcoski and Kratcoski (1975) used a modified revision of Short and Nye's (1958) questionnaire. The statistical analysis in this study is unsophisticated compared with, for example, the analysis by Weis (1975) and Jensen and Eve (1976), but Kratcoski and Kratcoski found that boys committed a wide range of offences with more frequency than girls. However, regarding the pattern of offending their study confirms the findings of other studies. Boys were more involved in 'aggressive' crimes — breaking into buildings, fist fights, destroying property, larceny of all types and joy-riding: 'However, on several items which have been postulated as particularly female delinquencies male—female differences were found to be slight. Distributions on several other items, which tend to reflect a teenage culture orientation — drinking, driving without a licence or permit, drug use, and skipping school — were about equal for boys—girls' (Kratcoski and Kratcoski, 1975, p.87).

Cernkovich and Giordano (1979) is one of the more recent and comprehensive comparative studies. They challenged one of the criticisms often levelled at self-report studies, namely that they often include very minor offences, by asserting that they needed to include these in their study as well as more serious offences, because it is these more minor offences that are usually attributed to females. They also used a number of items from the Short and Nye (1958) questionnaire. They conclude that their results show a high correlation between male and female offending. About 28 per cent (i.e. 10 out of 36) of the male—female differences were statistically non-significant. The remaining twenty-six offence types showed small but statistically significant differences between males and females. They suggest that the large sample (N = 822) probably contributed to the statistical significance of small differences. For each sex the rank-order correlation of offences was similar (as in Hindelang's, 1971a, study), the most frequent acts committed being the less serious, victimless status offences for both sexes. Acts least frequently engaged in were the more serious personal and property offences. Johnson's (1979) study also confirms that the rank-order of offences in his study was the same for males and females.

So far the studies reviewed have all been undertaken in the USA. There has been very little British research in this area to date and there is scope and need for much more. Campbell (1981) reports results from her 1976 study of urban working-class schoolgirls in Britain. Although not strictly a comparative study, she compares her data with West and Farrington's (1973) study of boys. In the thirty-eight-item list the correlation of admissions was +0.84. Campbell also reports Jamison's (1977) unpublished research on a sample of 781 boys and 501 girls from three areas in southern England. This research also showed a high correlation (+0.61) between boys and girls on offences.

Campbell (1981) re-worked the correlation on both her own and on Jamison's study to include only indictable offences, thus overcoming the criticism that the data includes minor offences which might bias the results. The re-worked correlations show for the Campbell and West and Farrington comparison a figure of +0.72 and for Jamison's study +0.80.

Another small British study, carried out in Bristol and Bath, England, between 1969 and 1972 supports the view that female delinquency was not mainly restricted to sexual misconduct as British official records, (also USA), would indicate (Shacklady-Smith, 1978). A self-report questionnaire was administered to three groups of girls: a probation sample (N = 15), a control sample (N = 30) and a gang sample (N = 15). A high proportion of the probation and gang samples admitted to deliberate property damage, namely gang fighting, joy-riding and breaking and entering. On the official records these offences accounted for only 8.9 per cent of offences in Bristol in 1970, whilst the care, protection and control offences accounted for 69.3 per cent of all cases that year.

Shacklady-Smith's (1978) research is not a comparative study and uses a very small sample, but nevertheless the results reflect the clear trend in the studies from the USA that the real pattern of female delinquency is very different from the pattern apparent from recorded statistics.

Mawby's (1980) research differs from other British studies and also from many of the American studies, in that his findings show significant gender differences in the pattern of delinquency in his Sheffield sample drawn from mainly working-class young people. He found differences significant at the 0.05 level on sixteen out of nineteen items. The three items showing no significant difference were thefts from school, thefts from others' houses and graffiti. He emphasizes the gender difference strongly in his conclusion, and whilst admitting that the difference is not as extreme as that found in official statistics, 'the most pronounced finding is the extent of difference rather than similarity' (ibid., p.536). One explanation for the differences found in this study and not reflected in others is that Mawby chose his categories of offence from those most common in the police files. If gender bias operates in the system, then it has already operated by the time an offence is reported in the police files and Mawby may well have found on a wider range of items that the differences were less than his data suggests.

Figueira-McDonough *et al.* (1981) report on one of the more recent American studies. Their survey involved 1735 males and females aged about 15 years in nine different schools in a mid-western county. Some of the data and their sample were comparable with Hindelang's (1971a) study and comparisons in trends over the decade are drawn; they conclude:

> our data support prior findings indicating differences by gender in the seriousness and frequency of delinquent involvement. It contradicts the notion tested in official statistics that females specialise in certain offences. It partially supports propositions that female and male delinquency have been converging over the last decade. Similarities are striking for subcultural offences and appear to have accentuated between 1969 and 1979. (Figueira-McDonough *et al.*, 1981, p.27)

They noted also that within the male group and the female group the rank-order of mean frequencies of delinquent involvement is very similar (Rs = 0.80).

Summary

The self-report studies summarized here vary in many ways: they cover a period of over twenty years across three decades; they involve a range of age, class and racial differences; they represent more and less sophisticated research techniques; and cover large and small samples. Also their geographical variety is apparent. Despite these differences — rather because of these differences — the accumulated evidence appears to be strongly in favour of the view that the *pattern* of male and female delinquency is more similar than was once believed and than official statistics still suggest. With regard to incidence, the accumulated evidence summarized in Table 2.1 shows that most studies verify that the *incidence* of delinquency is greater in males. Opinions as to the degree of that difference vary widely. Box (1983) suggests that the evidence is that serious conventional crime committed by females is fairly accurately represented in official statistics, but that less serious crime committed by juveniles is underrepresented. However, there is a degree of complexity to be considered in attempting to account for the differences between data from self-report studies and official statistics: a labelling theory approach would suggest that social definitions of sex roles influence the definition of crime; that chivalry and paternalism may well operate in police discretion at the decision to arrest and decision to prosecute; and differential reporting of crimes on a gender basis may well also be a factor. There is less empirical evidence of gender bias at these early stages in the judicial process, but there is a growing body of evidence that discrimination does operate at bail and sentencing stages. Nagel and Hagan (1983) summarize some of the evidence for adult females, and studies involving juveniles are summarized in the following section and in Table 2.8. If gender bias exists at these later stages of the judicial process, then it might be assumed that similar influences are at work in the initial stages and thus accounts for some of the differences between self-report data and official statistics. One factor clearly apparent from the self-report data is that official statistics overemphasize the sexual nature of female delinquency. Gender comparative studies of juveniles and the judicial process are reviewed in the following section in an attempt to explore further aspects of gender bias in the operation of the system.

II Gender comparative studies of the judicial system

Popular opinion, and often the opinions of professionals working in the police and in the probation and other welfare services, take the view that females are dealt with more leniently than males by the courts, and subscribe to the 'chivalry' view of female crime discussed in Chapter 1. Evidence which supports the view that gender bias does exist at various stages of the judicial process has been growing as a result of studies carried out over the past two decades. The following section of this chapter summarizes the main findings of these studies comparing the treatment of male and female juveniles at different stages in the judicial process, analyses the factors influencing these studies and assesses their contribution to understanding how female delinquents are treated by the courts. The summaries are treated in chronological order and it can be seen that some of the later studies build on the work done in the earlier ones. In comparison with other areas in criminology, this is a very under-researched area, and it is thought worthwhile to outline these few studies in some detail to enable comparison with the present study.

There were only two studies carried out before 1970 which compared the court dispositions of males and females. The earliest of these was that of Gibbons and Griswold (1957). This study involved all children referred to juvenile courts in Washington state from 1953 to 1955, involving over 18 000 children, the ratio of males to females being 3.5 : 1. Gibbons and Griswold found that non-white females were over-represented but this factor was not to be further explored until a much later study by Datesman and Scarpitti (1977). This Washington state study confirmed that females were concentrated in the status offences category, whilst males were concentrated in the theft and mischief categories. Girls were found to be more involved in sex offences than boys (9.8 to 4.7 per cent). Regarding dispositions, they found that girls' cases were slightly more likely to be dismissed than boys' (49.9 to 47.7 per cent), but that girls who received some other disposition were committed to institutions more often than boys. Gibbons and Griswold found that 11.3 per cent of the boys and 25.8

per cent of the girls whose cases were not dismissed were institution-alized. They conclude rather tentatively that because of other findings, such as girls more frequently coming from broken homes, the reader might conclude that the female sample is more maladjusted than the male sample. But they add a note of caution in drawing this conclusion, that none of the 'unfavourable' items in the findings characterized more than half of either boys or girls. It is perhaps a reflection of the date of this study that they attempt no further analysis of the differ-ences and particularly of the harsher policy of institutionalization towards the female sample. The larger numbers of studies carried out in the decade after 1970 are largely a result of increased awareness following the growth of the feminist movement and interpret their results in this light. One further study prior to 1970 was that under-taken by Cohn (1963), who studied 175 pre-sentence investigation reports presented to the judge of the Bronx district of New York's Children's Court during 1952.

The results showed a clear tendency for girls to be treated more harshly in their probation officers' recommendations: whilst girls were only one-sixth of the total group, they constituted about 50 per cent of those recommended for institutional care. This means that propor-tionally three times as many girls as boys were recommended for institutionalization. It is reported that cross-tabulation of the data for those females recommended for institutional care showed that the majority of them had committed offences involving sexual taboos. The conclusion that these were 'acts which were generally considered decisive factors in arriving at the recommendation they received' seems to imply that this is an acceptable situation. It is not discussed further in the paper, but is merely mentioned later in the context that sex, age and race seem to be more important than an individual approach to the young offender.

Although not a gender comparative study, the work of Tappan (1947) is remarkably enlightened considering the date of the research. He analysed the court records of 300 girls appearing in 1938 and 1942 and came to two main conclusions. The first was that sexual behaviour in the adolescent female can lead to exaggerated punitive treatment, and the second being that there is a fundamental conflict between the welfare and justice approaches which leads to 'confusion and deflection in the processes of adjudication and disposition' (ibid., p.159). Also although Terry's (1967) study was published before 1970, it fits better in philosophy and method with the later rather than the two earlier studies. It is a piece of research which was much quoted by later studies and possibly had a part in stimulating a number of them.

Terry (1967)

This study used data drawn from all offences on file during the years 1958–62 in an industrial mid-western community in the USA: 9023 offences were involved resulting in contact with police, 775 were referred to the probation department and 246 appeared in the juvenile court. Terry's study looked at the relationship of disposition with sex, race and socio-economic status at each of three levels of contact with the system: police, probation and the juvenile court. His findings contradicted the usual hypotheses in the literature. He found that severity of disposition was not a function of socio-economic status, or race, and that females were more severely sanctioned by the juvenile court, although sex differences were unimportant at the police and probation levels. Whilst not claiming to generalize from these data taken from a single community, he suggests that there is sufficient evidence to challenge existing assumptions and on which to base further research.

This study has the limitation that neither offence type nor prior record was controlled, so it is not possible to conclude what was the effect of status offences. Terry's findings stimulated a number of comparative studies of male and female delinquents being processed through the juvenile courts during the 1970s.

Chesney-Lind (1973)

Meda Chesney-Lind carried out a study of the case records and official court reports of the Honolulu Juvenile Court over a period of thirty-five years from 1929 to 1964. From a study of these records she concludes that, first, females are treated more harshly than males by the courts, which reflects the conclusions of Terry (1967); but her second major conclusion takes the case significantly further than either Terry or Cohn, in that she states that the court sexualizes female delinquency and that this is not the result of an intrinsic difference in the nature of female and male crime, but a result of the judicial process. Evidence is presented under four headings as follows.

The nature of the offences   Status offences accounted for 75.5 per cent of all female delinquency referrals but only 27.5 of male delinquency referrals. These figures contrast strongly with the similarity of male and female delinquency shown by self-report studies (e.g. Clark and Haurek, 1966; Wise, 1967; Jensen and Eve, 1976; Hindelang, 1969).

Court-ordered medical examinations   Clear differences were shown on a gender basis; for instance, in 1950, 12.2 per cent of male cases received a medical examination, against 78.6 per cent of female cases. The nature of the reports indicates the court's interest in the sexual activities of female juveniles. Often females referred for a criminal offence (e.g. car theft) were considered potential runaways and questioned about their sexual activity.

Detention Chesney-Lind's study shows clearly that females are more likely to be remanded in custody than males. In the study females constituted between 17 and 20 per cent of the court's total population for the years 1954—64. But they accounted for 30 per cent of admissions to the detention home. At any one time, females usually comprised 50 per cent of the detention home's population, and in the years 1954—64 the average length of stay for males was six days while for females the average stay was 15.6 days. The policy of the longer stay for females was so that 'for their own protection' they were given a more thorough investigation, thus (inevitably) other offences and problems would come to light.

Court disposals Over the period 1929—50 proportionately three times as many females as males were institutionalized, and this figure was maintained during the period 1954—64. In 1964 women constituted 20 per cent of delinquency referrals and 34 per cent of commitments to training school.

Chesney-Lind's position is strongly feminist and she concludes that 'the court's symbolic affirmation of old style morality by punishing adolescent females who violate or who might violate, the double standard serves as an important affirmation of the property status of all women' (1977, p.58). Whilst Cohn (1963) and Terry (1967) found that females were more harshly treated, they were less outraged and less questioning of the system which perpetuated this inequality. Kratcoski (1974), whilst acknowledging the double standard operated for males and females, accepts the 'chivalry' position in explaining the harsher treatment of females evident in his own study, namely that it is for their own well-being and protection that females are institutionalized more often than males.

Kratcoski (1974)

This study compared 682 males and 163 females appearing before the juvenile court, in 1971, in a mid-western state in the USA. It included a more detailed comparison of the offences than the studies cited so far, but contains no statistical analysis of the significance of these comparisons (Table 2.3).

Table 2.3 Kratcoski's comparison of male and female offending patterns

Type of most recent offence	Male (%)	Female (%)
Offence against property	58	36
Offence against persons	11	8
Truancy	9	24
Sex offence, runaway or incorrigibility	8	11
Other (curfew violation, disruptive school behaviour, etc.	14	21
Total	100	100

Source: Kratcoski, 1974, p.19.

It is concluded from this distribution of offences that the pattern of female offending is less serious than that of the male juveniles. It is noted particularly that there is a discrepancy in the figures for truancy. While it is generally recognized that truancy plays a significant part in male delinquency, Kratcoski suggests with caution that this might be a result of the double standard society operates for males and females, the caution being that he indicates there is some evidence that female delinquents truant more frequently than male delinquents though he quotes only one study in support of this argument, namely Gibbons and Griswold (1957).

Regarding the disposition of cases, Kratcoski's study showed that the court treated girls more harshly than boys. Although 69 per cent of boys committed delinquent acts as against 44 per cent of females, nevertheless 31 per cent of females and only 24 per cent of males were held in detention. Court officials explained this discrepancy that the juvenile court was a protective rather than a punishment agency, and the girls were often held for their own safety and well-being. Kratcoski appears to accept this position by concluding 'what may appear to be differential treatment of female offenders, may in fact be the juvenile court's response to girls' special needs and its utilization of the limited alternatives available' (p.20).

Hancock (1975)

This Australian study involved a sample of 300 male and 141 female court appearances in 1975; 63 per cent of the females were protection applicants against 8 per cent of the male sample. The remainder were brought on criminal charges.

The data from this study shows that regarding dispositions courts are more likely to choose probation, supervision or institution for girls (52 per cent females, 46 per cent males) and favoured bond, fine or adjournment for boys. Hancock sees the first group of disposals as rehabilitative and the second group as legislative. This could be interpreted that the courts are more severe with the boys. In fact most researchers would consider probation, supervision and institution to be the more severe sentences, though Hancock does not interpret her data in this way. When disposition was cross-tabulated with type of offence, she found that girls are treated less severely than boys but that when females offended against female standards they were more harshly treated than males. Although the analysis in this study could be clearer, it appears to support other studies indicating that status offenders in the female sample are more harshly treated.

With regard to the way in which female delinquency is defined, Hancock makes some interesting comments. In 40 per cent of female cases she found some reference to sex-appropriate behaviour, but in only 5 per cent of male cases. In 29 per cent of female cases sexual intercourse was mentioned but in only 1 per cent of cases in the male sample. In these instances sexual history was linked in male cases directly to a sex-related offence such as indecent exposure, while in the female sample sexual history was linked to the girl's attitude to authority, co-operation with the police, her credibility, home situation and moral reputation (Hiller and Hancock, 1981, p.119).

Cohen (1975)

This study of the Denver County Family Court found that females were less likely to be released by probation officials (40 to 50 per cent) and were also more likely to be placed on informal supervision (30 to 15 per cent).

Mann (1977)

This research, carried out in 1976, is reported in an unpublished PhD thesis submitted to the University of Illinois. Mann's sample consisted of 181 cases of which 81 were offenders (50 male, 31 female) and 100 were runaways or MINS cases (minors in need of supervision). The location was a mid-western urban county in the USA. It is different from most other similar studies in its data collection method which was from observation of court hearings over a period of two months using a structured checklist to aid the observation and recording. The sample was selected randomly; SPSS was the statistical package used for analysis of the data. Gender status was the independent variable and dependent variables were related to: social information; presence of parents in court; appearance and demeanour of the young person in court; type of offence committed; and presence of legal representative.

Results confirmed some findings of previous studies: for example, female status offenders were referred more frequently for medical examinations than were male status offenders, confirming Chesney-Lind's data (1973). In the case of both status respondents and delinquent respondents females were more often held in custody than were males thus confirming the data reported by Chesney-Lind, Cohn (1963), Kratcoski (1974) and May (1977). An interesting aspect of discrimination by the courts on a gender basis is reported by Mann and is not included in other studies: that is, the time spent on hearing the case. She found that in the MINS court significantly more time was allocated to male runaways (11 min) compared with time allocated to females (8.73 min). Similarly, in the delinquency cases the average time spent on hearing male cases was 10.9 min as compared with 9.4 min for female cases.

Mann's analysis of the comparison of offences between the male and female delinquent sample found less difference in the two samples than did May (1977); Table 2.4 shows the distribution of offences by sex. She points out that for the more serious offences — offences against the person — there is very little difference in the gender sub-samples, and it is in the less serious offences that the female sample is underrepresented. These data accord more closely with the self-report studies than do those of May.

With regard to court dispositions, Mann's data again confirms that girls may be dealt with more severely by the courts. This is particularly true in her MINS (status offenders) sample where the offence committed by both boys and girls was the same — all runaways. Table 2.5 shows dispositions by sex. In the delinquent sample, whilst the distribution of most severe dispositions was about the same between the gender sub-samples, females were less likely to receive the least severe disposition.

Mann's study, along with that of May (1977), are the two most comprehensive studies of the court process. However, Mann has little information about family background, though she has interesting data on race and on aspects such as time of hearings, parental attendance in court and legal representation not contained in other studies. Her statistical analysis, whilst fairly simple, is more sophisticated than some of the smaller studies reported in this section. Mann's data, and May's, serve as interesting cross-cultural comparisons — one British and the other American — and May suggests that some of the reasons

Table 2.4 Mann's data: distribution of offences, by sex

	Boys (%)	Girls (%)	
Personal offences			
Assault	1.2	6.2	
Battery	3.7	9.9	
Armed robbery	8.6	2.5	
Robbery	7.4	1.2	
Other	3.6	1.2	
Sub-total	24.5	21.0	
Property offences			
Theft	7.4	7.4	
Motor vehicle theft	7.4	2.5	
Burglary	16.0	3.7	
Other	6.4	3.7	
Sub-total	37.2	17.3	
Total	61.7	38.3	100

Source: Mann, 1977, p.173. table 22.

Table 2.5 Mann's data: court dispositions, by sex

| | MINS | | Delinquents | |
	Boys (%)	Girls (%)	Boys (%)	Girls (%)
Dispositions				
Most severe	18.0	28.0	50.0	41.9
Least severe	64.0	48.0	30.0	9.7
Other	18.0	24.0	20.0	48.4
	100.0	100.0	100.0	100.0

Source: Mann, 1977, p.129, table 8.

why his data is different from the American studies is a result of cultural differences. However, Australian studies (Leaper, 1974; Hancock, 1975; Fielding, 1977) also support the general tendency for females to be more harshly treated, particularly for status offences, for which they appear in greater proportion than males.

May (1977)

From an Aberdeen sample of 11 004 schoolchildren, in 1968, 126 female and 730 male delinquents were identified. May's findings on the comparison of the nature of female and male offences differ from some of the previous outlined studies. In this Aberdeen study he found that about 70 per cent of all female offences concerned property. He did not distinguish shoplifting as a separate offence, as indicated in his table II, reproduced here (Table 2.6).

Table 2.6   May's study: distribution of offences, by sex

Offence	Percentage of female offences	No. of girls charged with an offence per 100 boys
Theft	68.8	23
Breaking and entering	4.1	1
Vandalism	1.7	4
Breach of peace	9.5	22
Juvenile status offences	9.2	84
Sexual offences	1.3	12
Other offences	5.4	11

Source: May, 1977, p.205.

Status offences and sexual offences were not disproportionately represented as they are in studies carried out in the USA, but concerning court disposal the greater severity with regard to the female sample is clearly evident. May divides disposal into four categories: warning (conditional or absolute discharge); punishment (mainly fines); supervision; and detention. The warning category seems to have applied to the majority of offenders and evenly between the male and female sample (65.6 per cent male, 61.9 per cent female). However, in the remaining categories severe treatment of females is evident, especially so bearing in mind the less serious offences committed by the female sample. Females were less often fined (14 per cent female, 22 per cent male), more frequently placed on supervision (14 per cent female, 10 per cent male) and more likely to be sent to an institution (9 per cent female, 2 per cent male).

May's study is a comprehensive one, and he examines variables such as social disadvantage, area of residence, IQ and school attendance. However, he found that only age and offence show a strong positive association with disposal, but concedes that his findings show some support for the conclusions of Terry (1967), Cohn (1963) and Chesney-Lind (1973). The fact that status offences in this study constitute such a small proportion of the female sample — unlike other UK studies (Cowie, Cowie and Slater, 1968; Richardson, 1969) — is due to the fact that his was not an already institutionalized sample.

Datesman and Scarpitti (1977)

The sample was taken from 1103 juveniles appearing before a family court in an eastern city in the USA; it consisted of sub-samples of 200 females and 903 males. These sub-samples were also divided on a racial basis to include black and white juveniles. This study is one of the few to consider race as a dependent variable. The main focus of the study was to examine the relationship between sex and disposition whilst controlling for type of offence and previous record. Overall the data showed that females received harsher dispositions than males despite the fact that the female sample contained a higher percentage of first offenders: 68 per cent female, 54 per cent male (Table 2.7).

Table 2.7   Datesman and Scarpitti's data: court disposition, by sex

Disposition	Male (%)	Female (%)
Dismissed	9.2	7.3
Warned	34.1	33.3
Fined	10.0	1.7
Unsupervised probation	6.6	8.5
Probation officer	33.5	41.8
Public institution	6.6	7.3
Total	100.0	100.0

Source: Datesman and Scarpitti, 1977, p.304, table 1.

However when type of offence is introduced as a control variable, it emerges that for felonies and misdemeanours females are treated more leniently: 65 per cent of females and 32 per cent of males were dismissed or warned for felonies. In the case of status offences males are treated more leniently: 41 per cent of males and 17 per cent of females were dismissed or warned. Datesman and Scarpitti conclude that the juvenile court reinforces and perpetuates traditional and outmoded sex roles: 'In the final analysis the juvenile court appears to be less concerned with the protection of female offenders than the protection of the sexual status quo' (Datesman and Scarpitti, 1980, p.315).

Conway and Bogodan (1977)

Examination of the records of the New York State Family Court for the period 1965—74 showed that although several thousand fewer females were brought before the court for serious crimes, nevertheless, several thousand more females than males were placed in an institutional setting. The average percentage difference between the gender sub-samples for institutional placement over ten years was 9.2 per cent more females institutionalized. Datesman and Scarpitti (1977) noted that the difference in their sample was never more than 4 per cent. However, the sample was smaller and took account of only one year's figures. Conway and Bogodan examined the records for a comparison of the length of detention of males and females and found that throughout the ten-year period females are detained longer than males.

Sarri and Vinter (1978)

Although Sarri and Vinter's research is not a comparative study of the juvenile court, the National Assessment of Juvenile Corrections study of correctional programs supports the evidence found in the studies reported. Their evidence is important because it was based on a probability sample of 42 correctional programs in a universe of 922, thus drawing on a much wider sample than the studies already discussed. These data showed that females, regardless of offence, were more likely to be institutionalized. With regard to status and minor offences, they found that a high proportion of juveniles were institutionalized for these offences and particularly so for females. They noted further that consistently more males than females charged with school- or family-related offences were in day treatment centres.

Teilmann and Landry (1981)

Teilmann and Landry are critical of some of the studies carried out because they do not control for both offence type and prior record; they use their data to challenge the feminist position which several of the researchers in this area have been seen to take.

The data in this study was more extensive than in most: two sets of data were used to test gender bias at two levels in the system. The first set consisted of complete arrest histories collected on a random sample of cases arrested, in 1975, in California from the files of thirty-three police departments. The second set of data were collected from five states and consisted of referrals on the ground of status offences. This is significant because the resulting bias in this sample is probably underestimated by the researchers. However, the analysis is more sophisticated than in some of the other studies.

Analysis of the data showed considerable variety of practice in the different locations. No individual gender bias was noticed at any level of the system once previous offences and type of truant offence were controlled for. They suggest that where gender bias exists, it appears to be more against boys than girls, particularly in relation to delinquent offences. They concede, however, that female status offences are probably disproportionately represented in police, court and institutional populations (p.77), and that this is largely the result of the differing expectations which society has of boys and of girls. They propose that this difference is due more to parents than to the system since disposition decisions appeared to be not obviously and consistently biased. In most cases parents would be responsible for referring status offenders. This conclusion is probably inevitable because of the overrepresentation of status offenders within their sample and, therefore, needs to be treated with caution.

Webb (1984)

This is a survey of 14—16-year-olds who in 1978 were made subject to a supervision order for criminal offences. Information was collected from Social Inquiry Reports and care files of 241 girls and 971 boys in six high-delinquency areas in England and Wales. The data show that girls on supervision committed significantly less serious offences than boys, and that they were more likely to have been sentenced for being involved in one offence only, whereas the male delinquents had multiple offences; and 75 per cent of the female sample were first offenders, whereas only 46 per cent of boys were first offenders. Webb found no significant gender difference in the length of supervision order.

The recommendations in Social Inquiry Reports for supervision appeared not to be linked to a 'coherent welfare response' (p.372), and this applied equally to boys and girls. Hence Webb suggests that neither seriousness of offence nor history, or social 'need', appear to justify the recommendation, so concludes confidently that gender bias is evident — though to suggest that this is intentional gender bias is too crude an explanation.

Methodology

The methodology used in these studies varies a great deal. Some of them are more comprehensive such as May (1977), who introduces social variables, others are small in scope such as Casburn (1971), whilst still others such as Terry (1967) involve the use of a universe of 9023 offences. Other studies span a large period of time, thus Chesney-Lind's (1973) investigation covers thirty-five years of records in the Honolulu courts, whilst still others include a wide geographical span, thus Webb (1984) includes six locations in his research on supervision orders. The statistical sophistication of the studies varies a great deal too. Conway and Bogodan (1977) are criticized by Teilmann and Landry (1981) for working with numbers rather than percentages, Kratcoski (1974) does not apply simple bivariate analysis to his study which remains descriptive and a number of studies such as Cohn (1963), Terry (1967) and Chesney-Lind (1973) fail to control for nature of offence and previous offending record when comparing disposals of males and females. Some of the later studies such as Teilmann and Landry (1981) use a regression analysis, and Webb (1984) quotes precisely the significance levels in his study.

Although there may appear to be a number of these comparative studies, clearly this approach is methodologically in its infancy — and our knowledge of the area still tenuous. Further studies which are comprehensive in scope and methodologically strong are required to improve our knowledge in this field. Nevertheless, overall there is a striking consistency in the collective findings which should at least challenge complacency and lead us to question further the way in which female juveniles are processed in the courts.

Explanation of gender bias in juvenile justice

These summaries of research studies indicate collectively that gender bias operates at a number of stages in the judicial process, and these are summarized in Table 2.8. In the USA there is evidence of gender bias in the law itself, a number of states operating different age limits for males and females. An example is New York state, where in 1962 the Federal Juvenile Justice Law provided a non-criminal category for those aged under 16 who deviated from expectations. New York raised the 16 years age limit to 18 for girls or until they married with parental

Table 2.8 Summary table of reports and discussions of gender bias at various stages of the judicial process

1	Arrest	Monahan (1970); Teilmann and Landry (1981); Miller (n.d.)
2	Referrals	Gibbons and Griswold (1957); Datesman and Scarpitti (1977); Chesney-Lind (1978)
3	Pre-trial detention (remand in custody)	Mann (1977); Casburn (1971)
4	Probation officer's report	Cohn (1963); Cohen (1975)
5	Reasons for court appearance	Hancock (1975); Leaper (1974); Fielding (1977); Grichting (1977)
6	Use of court-ordered medical examinations and the sexualization of offences	Gold (1971); Chesney-Lind (1973); Hancock (1975); Mann (1977)
7	More severe court disposition	Gibbons and Griswold (1957); Cohn (1963); Terry (1967); Reiss (1960); Chesney-Lind (1973); Kratcoski (1974); Cohen (1975); Mann (1977); Conway and Bogodan (1977); Datesman and Scarpitti (1977); May (1977); Grichting (1977); Sarri and Vinter (1978); Webb (1984)
8	Time spent on court hearing	Mann (1977); Casburn (1971)
9	Length of detention	Velimesis (1975); Conway and Bogodan (1977); Sarri (1974); Armstrong (1977); Chesney-Lind (1978)
10	Parole	Hudson (1973); Velimesis (1975)

consent. The limit remained at 16 for boys (Conway and Bogodan, 1977; Sarri, 1976).

Clements (1972) in his review of sex and sentencing shows that the sentencing statutes applicable only to women were passed in most states at the turn of this century. Seven of the then ten states established the use of the indeterminate sentence for women, with all the attendant implications for civil rights and liberties. Velimesis (1975) demonstrates that in addition to other areas where differential treatment of girls is more severe than of boys is the revocation of parole for violation, as shown by Hudson (1973).

Armstrong (1977) argues that males and females are not equal under the law: sex is a significant determinant of the length and type of sentence and that this sometimes works in favour of, sometimes against, females' interests. She indicates that juvenile court statutes discriminate against females in different ways: they may establish higher juris-dictional age limits such as the example outlined above from the New York Family Court; several states in the USA allow for differences in permissible length of confinement for males and females, for example, females may be committed in New York to the state training school until age 20, but males must be released by the age 18; and until recently, she points out, Tennessee and Connecticut had special provisions in their codes referring only to females who may be committed to an institution for leading a 'vicious' or 'criminal' life. However, Armstrong points out that gender bias operates against men also. Examples she gives are that, under Arizona law, men are sentenced more severely than women when the victim of a crime is female, and under Oklahoma juvenile law, institutionalized delinquent females are discharged at 18, males at 21. An example from Macdonald is given to reinforce the existence of gender bias in the operation of the law: 'If a man walking past an apartment stops to watch a woman undressing before the window, he is arrested as a Peeping Tom. If a woman walk-ing past an apartment stops to watch a man undressing before the window, the man is arrested as an exhibitionist.'

One factor which is very clear in many of the court studies outlined is that juvenile females in the USA are overrepresented in the status offence categories. Chesney-Lind's (1973, 1974, 1977, 1978) has perhaps been the most vociferous explanation of why this is so; phrases such as 'judicial paternalism', 'the sexualisation of female crime' and 'the enforcement of a double standard of morality', give some indi-cation of the force with which her position is set out. However, her arguments are persuasive and well supported by evidence. Chesney-Lind (1977) points out that although females constitute only about 25 per cent of the young people dealt with in juvenile courts in the USA, they may be a majority of those charged with status offences, for instance, running away from home, 'incorrigibility', 'waywardness', and so on. Self-report studies, as has been seen in the previous section of this chapter, demonstrate that the level of delinquency is more similar in male and female juveniles than the official statistics might suggest, and so the difference in the number of males and females processed for status offences arises largely out of differential expectations for male and female children in the traditional family. Sons are allowed to 'sow wild oats', whilst girls' behaviour is closely monitored:

> From their sons, parents expect achievement, aggressiveness and indepen-dence, but from their daughters, obedience, passivity and implicitly, chastity. The female sex-role is more restrictive than its male counterpart. (Chesney-Lind, 1978, p.173)

The juvenile justice system supports this dual standard, thus a 'de facto double standard of justice' is created, argues Chesney-Lind. It enforces not only the law, but a double standard of morality. Chesney-Lind (1973) asserts that because female delinquency is perceived as a threat to these standards, it explains why, first, the juvenile court system selects out those aspects of female deviance which violate sex-role expectations rather than those which violate legal norms, and secondly, why female delinquency, and especially sexual delinquency, is viewed more seriously than male delinquency and punished more severely. She further illustrates from arrest and detention statistics how the system develops a 'judicial paternalism' which operates against the interest of girls: one such example is the routine, indiscriminate medical including a gynaecological examination of all girls appearing before the family court in New York or in many institutions as part of the admission process whether their offences were sexual in nature or not. Gold (1971), Hancock (1975) and Mann (1977) also confirm this practice in their studies. Practice in the UK has reflected this approach also, although it has not been documented in research studies. Richardson's (1969) study of institutionalized female delinquents in Britain recognizes the issue in a passing reference:

> Those who were hardly touched emotionally (by their sexual experiences) were often disturbed much by the aftermath and doubtless the subsequent enquiries, physical examinations (often physical treatment) and court evidence served to magnify and distort their experiences which were so clearly disproportionate for girls of their age. (ibid., p.219)

One illogical outcome of this — or it may be the view influencing such practice — is that girls are more likely to be labelled as 'carriers' of venereal disease than are boys.

Thus it can be seen that a much narrower range of acceptable behaviour applies to girls and they receive harsher treatment for non-criminal offences than do boys who have broken the law because, argues Chesney-Lind from a feminist position, female delinquency challenges the authority of the family, the viability of the double standard and the maintenance of the present system of sexual inequality.

Sarri (1976) also takes a feminist position in attempting to explain the gender bias evident in the judicial system and suggests that it operates at two levels: that it is inherent within state laws in the USA, and that it is present in the attitudes and ideologies of those administering the law, often intended to be protective, since there is a dominance of male staff in critical decision-making posts in juvenile justice agencies. Sarri pursues the argument further by asserting that female juveniles are not detained for the protection of the community since 55 per cent are detained for status offences, 17 per cent drug offences, 13 per cent property offences and 12 per cent person-related offences (ibid., p.78), yet they are placed in institutions more frequently and detained for longer periods. She concludes: 'All society is being harmed by a serious overkill in the processing of females, and in the long run the society will be irreversibly harmed' (ibid., p.79).

Hiller and Hancock (1981) draw on a different line of explanation from the feminist position of Armstrong, Chesney-Lind and Sarri since they suggest that female juveniles have become the victims of the 'welfare' approach. They draw on Platt's (1969) analysis of the growth of the child-saving movement as in part a need to restrict the independence and autonomy of young people. The welfare approach or 'treatment' model tends to result in a stronger response to delinquency since it encourages the use of indeterminate sentences, and the idea of 'potential' delinquents and the early identification and thus labelling of youngsters who may become delinquent. In the UK after the implementation of the Children and Young Persons Act 1969, it was noted that more young people received custodial sentences: in fact the welfare orientation of this Act had intended a more lenient approach (May, 1971). One disadvantage of the 'medical' model as a response to delinquency is that it 'diverts our attention from the critical role that social audiences play in defining behaviour as delinquent or non-delinquent' (Balch, 1975, p.116). Balch asked seventy-five social welfare students to evaluate the care of a 15-year-old who had had sexual intercourse with a number of partners, but appeared unconcerned about the possibility of pregnancy:

> When I identified the child as male, most respondents said either that no action whatsoever should be taken or that the boy's parent should simply be told about his behaviour, but when the respondents believed the child was a girl, over 75% said she should be referred to a mental health clinic for psychiatric help. (ibid., p.119)

Therefore, the social context is seen to be important in the definition of delinquent acts, and as the above example shows, gender bias is part of that social context. Evidence of bias to the treatment response is seen in May (1977), 'where the girl was perceived to be in some kind of moral danger, the courts were inclined to adopt more *positive* action' (p.210). The 'positive' action was for the females to be placed on supervision or institutionalized. Another dimension of the social content of delinquent behaviour is explored by Datesman and Scarpitti (1977), who showed that middle-class white girls were treated more severely for status offences than lower-class black girls because presumably they had deviated from role expectations.

Thus these mainly American studies show that gender bias operates at a number of levels in the judicial process and differing explanations are offered: it may result from strong and deeply held traditional views embedded in our social system about family authority, sexual morality and adolescent behaviour, and the way in which these values influence those who implement the system; or it may be the result of the more evident trend throughout this century to a more welfare- and treatment-oriented as opposed to a justice model in responding to juvenile delinquency. The likelihood is that both of these factors are operating in the same direction to create a powerful and insidious gender bias in the system.

Female juveniles in the British courts

It might well be argued that since the majority of studies discussed in this section are American, the conclusions are not valid in the UK. There are very few British studies comparing male and female delinquents appearing before the juvenile court. Casburn (1979) carried out a small observation study of young people aged 12–17 appearing before a juvenile court in a London borough over a period of 12 weeks: 208 young people were dealt with, of whom 28 were girls; 22 of the girls appeared on non-criminal charges, mostly truancy and care proceedings on the grounds of being 'in moral danger' or 'beyond control'. Only one male appeared on care proceedings grounds and he was a 6-month-old baby. This would seem to reflect the overrepresentation of females appearing for status offences in the American studies. Casburn argues that the dispositions seemed more severe and reflected the findings in Terry's (1967) research. Although many of the boys appearing had a history of offending, only five out of 168 received a disposal involving institutional care. There were no care orders passed on boys. In contrast, argues Casburn, two white girls on their first court appearance received care orders and two black girls received two-year supervision orders; 25 per cent of the female sample were remanded in care and females were more often remanded for full reports including psychiatric and psychological assessment than were the boys. Whereas Mann (1977) found that a shorter time was spent on hearing girls' cases, Casburn found that the magistrates spent longer. Casburn admits that her study is impressionistic. It deals with small numbers in the juvenile court and makes no attempt at a statistical analysis of the data. She is concerned to demonstrate that the court reflects, supports and perpetuates the socio-legal status of women in society. This she does indeed do, supported with illustrations from the history of the development of the juvenile court.

May (1977) and Webb (1984) are the two most substantial British studies, summarized earlier. May suggests that some of the findings of his Aberdeen study correlate with some of the American studies and, in particular, disprove the view that female offences are predominantly sex-related or that the broken home is a prominent feature of the social background. He does, however, argue for caution in cross-cultural comparisons. Webb concluded from his research covering six geographical areas and a rigorous statistical approach that gender bias was evident in British juvenile courts. What is clearly needed are further comprehensive comparative studies of male and female juveniles being processed by the juvenile court, which takes into account social background, nature of offence and court disposition. The present study aims to do this.

There are one or two studies, which although not comparative have shed light on the way in which female delinquents are dealt with by the courts. Davies (1976) includes useful information about the nature of offences and family and social background, but because it is not a comparative study contributes little to a study of gender bias. Similarly, Tappan's (1947) classic study has not been considered in detail in this review for the same reason; nevertheless, his comment on the severity of treatment of female offenders is all the more interesting bearing in mind the date of his research:

> In searching for the reason for this disparity between conduct and disposition, one is led to two general conclusions about the handling of Wayward Minors: in the work of the court in general, sex behaviour on the part of an unmarried or pre-adult girl looms as an offence of great gravity which can lead to exaggerated punitive treatment. (ibid., p.159)

The second general conclusion he referred to was the incompatibility he saw between a justice and a welfare approach.

With regard to British commentaries on issues relating to juvenile offenders and the courts, there are few who treat females in any detail. An exception is Gelsthorpe (1981), whose examination of policy appears to be set in the context of the acceptance of pathological and psychological explanations of delinquency in girls (p.6). She argues that the sentencing pattern of boys and girls in British juvenile courts is very similar. Had she examined this evidence against the nature of the offences committed, it is likely she would have found that the girls' group had less serious offences, and so a similar sentencing pattern to that of boys would indicate a more severe treatment of females. Smart (1976) and Rutter and Giller (1983) also contain brief accounts of female juvenile delinquency, reference to relevant research and the main issues.

Because the British research and comment in this area is so limited to date, the present study aims to explore gender bias at two levels: at the level of police discretion by examining the functioning of the juvenile consultative panels, and at the level of the juvenile court. Male and female dispositions are compared at both levels, controlling for nature of present offence and also previous history of the young person. In addition, the section on the juvenile court examines the social background of the young offender.

III Gender and social background

Since the publication in 1947 of Bowlby's study of forty-four juvenile thieves, and his subsequent presentation of a report to the World Health Organization (1951), the concept of maternal deprivation has been the subject of numerous research studies and has had a far-reaching impact on child care services and policies. In his 1947 study Bowlby made popular the view that maternal deprivation is one of the most important factors in the aetiology of delinquency.

Rutter's (1972) review of subsequent research led him to modify the conclusions reached by Bowlby: he questioned the use of the umbrella term 'maternal deprivation' to cover a range of situations since the evidence suggests that lack of care or distortion of care are more important than loss, and that greater damage occurs where bonds fail to develop in the first place. Rutter also drew attention to the area of individual differences in response to parental deprivation, and to the fact that very few studies explored gender differences in vulnerability to these conditions.

Research by Andry (1960) examined paternal deprivation. This later study, however, laid less emphasis on uni-causal explanations of delinquent behaviour, and also took into account the differing effects of physical and psychological separation. Bandura and Walters (1958), Janes (1958) and McCord, McCord and Thurber (1962) also focus on the role of the father, and suggest a significant relationship between lack of an adequate father-figure and delinquency. Lang, Papenfuhs and Walters (1976) focus particularly on the fathers of female delinquents and found them to be generally ineffective in their role.

Both Bowlby and Andry are representatives of numerous studies in the psychodynamic tradition, many focusing on broken homes more generally and establishing a link between deprivation of either or both parents and delinquency in the child. Many of these studies pre-date Bowlby by many years: he confirmed and popularized ideas which had been around for some time, for example, Schideler (1918), Slawson (1923) and Bushong (1926) were very early studies on this theme, and Burt (1925) incorporated such ideas in his classic study. Later studies too confirmed the very strong association between broken homes and delinquency. The Gluecks (1952) discovered that parental deprivation occurred twice as often in their sample group of 500 delinquent boys than in their matched control group. Bennett (1960) in her comparison of delinquent and neurotic children found that parental separation occurred more frequently in the delinquent group than in the neurotic group. Ainsworth (1962) found that stealing was more frequent amongst children in his study who came from broken homes than amongst those who came from intact homes; and in Little's (1965) study only one-fifth of cases had not been separated from their parents.

One of the most recent and comprehensive reviews of research on the psycho-social correlates of delinquency has been undertaken by Rutter and Giller (1983). Family variables which they identify as being associated with delinquency are: parental criminality; poor parental supervision, cruel, passive or neglecting attitudes and erratic or harsh discipline; and marital conflict and large family size. They suggest that there is evidence that these variables apply across a range of social and ethnic groups, and they guard against the criticism that these family variables may be the outcome rather than the cause of delinquent behaviour by focusing mainly on studies where the data on families were collected prior to conviction.

Rutter and Giller review the research evidence also for other variables and their association with delinquency such as: social class; race; television; school influence; geographical area, particularly in relation to the difference between urban and rural settings; and conditions of the physical environment such as housing design and household density.

With this plethora of research available on the possible correlation between broken homes and juvenile delinquency, it is surprising that very few of the studies have been gender comparative. The studies mentioned above are mainly ones which focus on males or in which, if females are included in the sample, no comparison is made on a gender basis in reporting the results. There have, however, been a few significant studies and these are reviewed in more detail under three headings: the effect of broken homes on male and female juvenile delinquents; socio-economic status and other miscellaneous variables such as family size and geographical area; and group participation in delinquent behaviour.

Broken homes: gender comparative studies

One of the earliest studies is Weeks (1940), which differs from the prevailing view that there is a higher incidence of broken homes in female delinquent populations than there is in male delinquent groups. In his sample of 420 males and 95 females taken from the records of a juvenile court in Washington state the incidence of broken homes in the male sample was 39.6 per cent and in the female sample 68.1 per cent. It was hypothesized that this gender difference is not a real one and can be explained depending on the offence for which the young person was referred. In a gender comparison controlling for type of offence it was found that the significance in the difference disappeared, and it was concluded that the higher incidence of broken homes in female delinquent populations is a function of the type of offence for which they are most commonly referred, that is, status offences, ungovernability and running away from home. Only two other gender comparative studies support these findings: Grygier et al. (1969) found no significant difference in their training school samples of male and female delinquents with regard to the incidence of parental deprivation. They also emphasize the danger of focusing on the pathology of one or other parent, and warn that whilst their data measure incidence of parental deprivation, it is insufficient to draw from this conclusions about its role as a cause of delinquency. The third gender comparative study to find no significant difference in male—female groups with regard to broken homes is one which set out to follow up Weeks's (1940) conclusions. Datesman, Scarpitti and Stephenson (1975) found that the marital status of parents was weakly related to sex when type of offence is not controlled (12 per cent difference between male and female groups). When type of offence is taken into consideration, they found that the difference between male and female groups was insignificant for person or property offences, but in a comparison of males and females charged with ungovernability and running away the difference again became significant: 55 per cent of the males came from broken families, and 68 per cent of the females.

Although not a direct comparative study, Riege (1972) used her study of institutionalized female delinquents as a comparison with Andry's (1960) study of institutionalized male delinquents. Riege asserts that in neither study did statistically significant findings emerge 'regarding the number of separations from parents, age at separation, or of duration of separation that differentiated between delinquents and non-delinquents' (p.70).

An important gender comparative study of delinquency and broken homes which also controls for type of offence is Monahan (1957a), which examines data relating to all delinquency cases disposed of by the Philadelphia Municipal Court during the years 1949—54. The cases numbered 44 448. These data showed that the range of broken homes extended from one-third of the white boys' group to three-quarters of the black girls' group, with white girls showing less than 50 per cent with intact families. When offences were controlled for in the girls' sample, the data show the same high proportion of broken homes despite the offence. In a further report Monahan (1957b) suggests that when sex and colour are controlled, there has been no increase in the overall proportion of broken homes over the period 1916—56, however there is a change in the nature of the broken home involving a drop in orphanhood, an increase in mother-only families and an increase in socially broken families from divorce or separation. Thus whilst Monahan's first (1957a) report confirms the high incidence of broken homes amongst the female delinquent group, his second (1957b) report suggests that the data give no support to the belief in the overriding importance of the socially broken home in delinquent patterns.

Another study which showed very strong gender differences was that of Wattenberg and Saunders (1954) in their report of research undertaken from data of the Police Youth Bureau in Detroit, in 1952, on 3451 boys and 1082 girls. Their data showed strong differences between the sexes and they emphasize the statistically high significance in the results produced. Other variables were also significantly different in this study, namely offences, family relations, peer group relations and socio-economic factors. Gibbons and Griswold (1957) set out to test the findings of the Wattenberg and Saunders study. Their examination of over 18 000 cases referred to the juvenile court in Washington state during 1952 and 1953 also confirmed a higher incidence of broken homes in the female sample: 57.3 per cent of boys and only 42.2 per cent of girls were living with both parents. When offences were controlled for, differences were still noted but in the running away and ungovernable category the percentage of boys living with both parents fell to 42.2 per cent and that of the girls to 36.6 per cent. It should be noted that these figures are closer to the results of Weeks (1940), Grygier *et al.* (1969) and Datesman, Scarpitti and Stephenson (1975), although Gibbons and Griswold include an unqualified insistence in their conclusion that girls are more likely to come from broken homes.

One limitation which the above studies have in common is that they include no control group as a comparison. Morris's (1964) study did include both male and female non-delinquent control groups, and confirmed that the delinquent girls had the highest incidence of broken homes and families where there are overall family tensions. Morris interprets these findings by suggesting that if one accepts that delinquency occurs when culturally defined success is impossible to achieve (cf. Merton, 1938), then because female success is defined more in terms of the achievement and maintenance of positive affective relationships then also female delinquents will inevitably come from broken homes more frequently than males, whose success is defined culturally in terms of power and status. Furthermore, argues Morris, this interpretation would also explain why there are less female delinquents than males because the legitimate means of achieving their goals are more available to boys than girls. However, this explanation must be viewed as questionable in the light of evidence from self-report studies outlined in an earlier part of this chapter.

Other studies such as that of O'Kelly (1965), Andrew (1976) and Caplan et al. (1980) confirmed the view that female delinquents more often come from broken families. Andrew uses her data to explain the growth of female delinquency, that is, because there is an increase in divorce statistics, there will be an increase in female delinquency. This explanation, however, is ill-based since it makes the mistake of assuming that incidence is synonymous with cause.

Thus the prevailing view in these gender comparative studies is that female delinquents more often come from broken homes, but there is evidence also that the gender difference may not be as significant as is often claimed. One factor which has tended to overemphasize the importance of the broken home in relation to female delinquents is those studies which have been carried out on already institutionalized female delinquents. Trèse (1962) found that 73 per cent of delinquents studied were from broken homes, and Koller's (1971) Australian study showed that 61.5 per cent of the training school group had experienced parental loss and a further 32 per cent had experienced lengthy separations.

Lukianowicz (1971) found that all the girls in his sample, with the exception of one, came from an emotionally disturbed and unstable home but found that only 38 per cent came from a broken home. This compares with Cowie, Cowie and Slater's (1968) sample of 46 per cent from a broken home. Unusually both these studies are British.

Cockburn and Maclay (1965), in another rare British study of 50 boys and 50 girls in two remand homes in London, found that broken homes occurred more frequently in the female sample: the girls' mothers were less affectionate and gave less suitable supervision, whilst the boys' families were described as more 'cohesive'.

Gilbert's (1972) study attempted to use variables associated with quality of parenting as a predictive factor in delinquency in her comparison of approved school and secondary modern school girls. She found that the value of the variable separation from parents as a predictive factor was qualified by factors such as affection and discipline. This evidence would also seem to support that of Wattenberg and Saunders (1955). In these studies of institutionalized subjects we see the problem that incidence is confused with cause, though not necessarily by the researchers themselves, by interpretations put on the collective evidence. Many female delinquents in institutions are of course placed there because of family problems pre-existing the offence.

Further work is, therefore, needed on female delinquency and broken homes which is methodologically more rigorous than past studies. Studies need to be gender comparative; to use matched control groups of non-delinquents; to control for type of offence; and not use already institutionalized samples. But there is sufficient evidence to suggest that we should query a too easy and straightforward association between broken homes and female delinquency.

Socio-economic status: gender comparative studies

One of the earliest gender comparisons of juvenile delinquents taking socio-economic status into account was that of Wattenberg and Saunders (1954). Their study showed very significant differences over a range of variables between males and females. They found more girls than boys in both the lowest and highest social class groups: 'the curves of distribution for socio-economic variables tended to be flat for the girls and peaked, with a concentration near average for the boys' (p.29). As their research included no non-delinquent control groups, they include a caveat regarding the interpretation of the results.

Although there were few gender comparative studies, the association between delinquency and low or working class was generally accepted. However, the increased use of the self-report study — some of which were also gender comparative — challenged these views.

Nye, Short and Olson (1958) tested the null hypothesis that there is no significant difference in the delinquent behaviour of boys and girls in different socio-economic strata. Using a self-report questionnaire to indicate delinquent behaviour, and father's occupation to indicate social status, their survey of 2865 boys and girls did not show sufficient difference to reject the null hypothesis. Their hypothesis was re-tested by Akers (1964), who confirmed similar results. Dentler and Monroe (1961) also found no association between theft and socio-economic status in their study. Clark and Wenninger (1962) failed to detect any significant difference in the social class of delinquents in their study, but they raised the question that if the results of recent self-report studies are true, then the theoretical formulations regarding the aetiology of delinquency which rely heavily on the assumption that most delinquents are working class, such as Merton (1938), Miller (1958), Cohen (1955) and Cloward and Ohlin (1960), is brought into question. They resolved this, however, by suggesting that there is a difference between areas and the incidence of delinquency. Voss (1966) gathered his data which was gender comparative in Honolulu, and although there were cross-cultural complications in interpreting the data, he supported the view that area is more important than socio-economic status. He found no significant difference between males and females in respect of class distribution, nor did May (1977) in his British gender comparative study. Two studies show some disagreement with the self-report studies but both used official statistics: the first, Kashani *et al.* (1980), used those of a juvenile court in the USA, and the second, Wilson (1975), those of families known to a British social services department. Kashani *et al.* found that the socio-economic status of girls in their study was higher than that of the boys. Wilson, inevitably perhaps bearing in mind the source of the data, found social handicap a significant factor for the boys and girls in her study. Lucianowicz (1972) in a study of institutionalized females found that three-fifths came from social class 5. Similarly, these results should not be surprising bearing in mind the source of the data.

Thus the research outlined shows no significant difference between the sexes regarding distribution of delinquency according to socio-economic status. This brief review of research does, however, highlight the different results from self-report studies and from studies using official sources of data.

Other variables related to social background: gender comparisons

Barker and Adams's (1962) research compared a small group of 77 girls with 124 boys in two state training schools in the USA. Whilst they found clear differences in the offences committed between the two groups, they found no significant difference in family composition and variables they called 'personal disorganisation in the mother and in the father'. Cockburn and Maclay (1965) in a small British study similarly found no gender difference in respect of family size, religion, home state, IQ or working mothers. An unexpected finding in view of the interpretation given to female delinquents as 'disturbed' rather than deviant is that the boys in their group had more physical handicaps and psychiatric symptoms than the girls' group. However, the numbers in this study (50 males, 50 females) make generalization impossible. Hindelang (1976) pursued a different theme in questioning assumptions about the group nature of delinquent behaviour. Some theories of delinquency are built on the assumption that delinquency is a group phenomenon, for example, Cohen (1955), Matza (1964), Cloward and Ohlin (1960), Downes (1966) and Yablonsky (1962). Hindelang's (1971b) research on the same subject had focused only on urban males, but in his later study he included a gender comparison and also an urban–rural comparison. He found that urban and rural males had similar group involvement, whilst urban females more often committed offences in company than did urban males and rural females more often acted alone than did rural males. He suggests from this self-report study that 'substantial percentages' of delinquent acts are committed by individuals acting alone.

Andrew's (1976) research suggested that male delinquents were more likely to come from larger families than females, but Koller's (1971) study of females showed that they came only from larger than average families, with younger than average parents. However Offord et al. (1979) produced results in agreement with Andrew. Offord et al. also produced interesting data with regard to parental mental illness: they found that it was significant only in their delinquent group, and only in relation to mothers. They also found that their delinquent group were more likely to have parents with a criminal record.

A more recent piece of research by Caplan et al. (1980) produced data which are very interesting. They compared male and female cases referred to a family court clinic in Toronto and included 1050 males and 382 females. Their results showed significant gender difference for some variables, namely offences charged, delinquency and referral history, symptoms and problem behaviours, delinquents' personal histories and school histories, and socio-economic factors. For other variables there was no significant gender difference, namely family size, ordinal position adoption patterns, area of residence, type of housing, marital status of parent, father's age or education and employment. Caplan et al. point out that most gender comparative studies tend, as theirs does, to focus on explanations of gender difference, but they argue the gender similarities may well carry equal significance.

It will be apparent from the research reviewed in this chapter under the heading 'Incidence and pattern of delinquency' that there are gender similarities which, in turn, carry significance for the differential treatment of females in the courts. It is apparent from the third section on 'Social background', where gender comparative studies are few, that further research is required.

The present study aims to cover each of these areas: the nature of offences and offending patterns; the treatment of juveniles at two stages in the process — the consultative panels and the juvenile courts; and also to look at some aspects of social background of the young offenders. Each of these areas are examined in respect of gender comparisons. Although the scale of the research is small, it is hoped that its comprehensiveness and its location in the UK — most existing studies have been carried out in the USA — will contribute to its usefulness.

3 The present study: research method

The present study was designed to examine possible gender bias in the differential treatment of male and female offenders in the UK at two stages in the juvenile justice system. The first of these stages was the police cautioning stage, which in the research locations was carried out with reference, first, to a consultative panel on which social services, the probation service and the education welfare service were represented. The second stage at which possible differential treatment of cases according to gender was examined, was the juvenile court stage. In all, the study consisted of 399 cases, comprising 200 male and 199 female.

The literature review in the previous chapters has indicated that many previous gender comparative studies on court dispositions have failed to control for variables such as type of offence, or age, or other factors. The independent variable in the present study was gender, and the dependent variables were the recommendation of the consultative panel and the disposition of the juvenile court. A number of intervening variables were examined and included: age; previous and present pattern of offending, including type and value of offence, and whether the offence was committed alone or with friends or siblings; the recommendations, if any, in a social inquiry report; plea; and the frequency and nature of comments by agencies participating in the consultative panels. A further group of variables was included concerning the socio-economic status of the cases involved in the study. These included: social class, the employment pattern of the young person and parents; known parental criminal record, if any; number of siblings and their delinquent record, if any; family structure; and substitute care.

Thus although the numbers involved in the present study are small, and the cases were drawn from only two locations, nevertheless the study offers a more comprehensive basis for examining possible differential treatment, on the basis of gender, of juveniles in the justice system. Its location in the UK is also important since it will be apparent from the literature review that the majority of studies have been carried out in the USA.

Research hypotheses were formulated based on traditional assumptions about the nature of female juvenile delinquency:

1   That gender is a significant factor in decision-making at two stages of the process of juvenile justice, in that girls are treated more leniently than boys
    (a)   in police decisions to prosecute;
    (b)   in the dispositions of the juvenile court.
2   That male and female juveniles will differ significantly with regard to the nature and pattern of offending.
3   That location differences between small town and city delinquents will show that female delinquency in the city is more serious than in the small town.
4   That there will be significant differences in the social background of young male and female offenders; more females would be expected to come from broken homes.

Geographical location of the research

The research took place in two centres as follows.

City location A is a major coastal city with a population of approximately 300 000. It is a civic and cultural centre for the region, and also a commercial and trading centre in character with its role as a port; location A is also a university city. Like most cities, it has deprived areas in the inner city with many social problems in evidence, and middle-class suburbs on the outskirts. Unemployment was significant at the time of the research (at 11.6 per cent of the population, 9.8 per cent being the national average) owing to the closure of one of the steelworks situated there.

Town location B is a town situated 25 miles from the city location A, and has a population of approximately 54 000. It borders on the industrial belt surrounding the city and on a rural expanse of Outstanding Natural Beauty. In tradition and culture the town is associated more with industry than with the tourism which is an important feature in the life of towns not far away. Location B is steeped in its lively political history and the left-wing traditions still permeating the life of the town today are fuelled by the high unemployment rate (12.1 per cent of the population at the time of the research). Coalmining, iron and steel and other major industries of the area are in serious decline and funding from central government and from the European Economic Community has attracted as yet only a few new industries to the area. Whilst socially location B has had a tradition of close-knit families and community and neighbourhood support, there now exist a number of social problems, many of these located on two large council housing estates in the town.

The two locations in which the research took place are situated within different county boundaries, and so come within a different administrative area for probation, social services and the local education authority. Both locations come within the same police area.

The consultative panels

The consultative panels in the police area in which the research took place were set up in 1976, and had been in operation for about five years at the time of the research. They were established in response to a Home Office recommendation to police forces throughout the country to consult with welfare agencies before making a decision to charge a juvenile offender. Their establishment was in the spirit of the welfare orientation of the Children and Young Persons Act 1969. Many police forces now operate some similar kind of arrangement for consultation, although some forces still make the decision to charge, then merely inform, rather than consult with, the other agencies. The status of the panels are consultative, and in the area of the research the panel made a recommendation to the police superintendent with whom the final decision rested. In the present sample, in only three cases out of 200 did the superintendent make a decision which differed from the panel recommendation.

The panels met regularly and frequently in both locations in which the research took place; they were chaired by a police sergeant responsible for juvenile liaison. The Education Welfare Department of the local education authority was represented on the panels, as were the probation service and social services. In the town location the composition of the panel was fairly consistent as one representative from each agency was able to represent the area, being geographically smaller than the city location. This continuity fostered a spirit of co-operation and trust. The composition of the city panels was wider involving, for example, more than one Education Welfare Officer because of the

number of areas in the city to be covered. Since the panel recommendation is accepted in most cases by the police superintendent, then
clearly the way in which these bodies come to their decisions is of
interest in any exploration of gender bias, and hence their inclusion in
the present study.

Data collection

In each location permission was obtained for access to the data and
for assistance in data collection from five agencies: the magistrates'
courts, the police, the social services department, the probation service
and the Education Welfare Service of the local education authority.
Data collection began late in 1980 with the courts, social services and
probation in location B, followed by data collection from the courts,
social services and probation in location A. Forms were completed by
the Clerk of the Court (Appendix I) in each location and passed on by
the Clerk's department to either social services or probation, depending
on which service had responsibility for the case. In most cases juveniles
over age 13 were referred to probation, but there are exceptions
where cases were clearly known to social services and where there was
continuing work by them with the family concerned. A form on socio-
economic status and background (Appendix II) was completed for each
case by the probation officer or social worker having responsibility
for the case in most cases, although a number of these forms were
completed from records by the researcher where pressure of time and
work had meant that the worker involved with the area had not been
able to complete the form. Data collection for the juvenile court
phase of the research was completed by June 1982. The length of
time for data collection in this section was governed by the rate at
which girls appeared in court in location B, and in order to achieve
a sub-sample of 50 cases data were collected retrospectively on a small
number of cases (see Table 3.1a for dates).

Table 3.1a   Data collection: phases 1 and 2, juvenile courts

	Town	City
Male	September 1980 to March 1981	June 1981 to February 1982
Female	January 1979 to August 1981	June 1981 to May 1982

Data collection for the consultative panels was carried out by a juvenile liaison police sergeant in each location and who was also chairman of the panel. A form (Appendix III) was completed for each case, and Table 3.1b shows the dates of panel sittings and the number of cases drawn from each over the data collection period. As with the juvenile court sample, the timespan for the data collection was determined by the rate of referral of female cases in town location B where the rate of female referrals was obviously slower than in the city. After a pilot study, the forms were completed retrospectively in the spring of 1982.

Table 3.1b   Data collection: phase 2, consultative panels

	Location A			Location B	
Panels sitting on	No. of male cases	No. of female cases	Panels sitting on	No. of male cases	No. of female cases
7.4.81	16	7	6.4.81	2	4
			7.4.81	3	3
			13.4.81	3	1
14.4.81	2	2	14.4.81	1	1
21.4.81	2	3	27.4.81	2	0
28.4.81	15	9	28.4.81	1	1
			5.5.81	9	8
			12.5.81	0	2
19.5.81	0	2	18.5.81	4	4
26.5.81	0	4	1.6.81	0	2
2.6.81	0	12	8.6.81	2	2
9.6.81.	15	11	9.6.81	4	4
			15.6.81	3	1
			16.6.81	4	4
			23.6.81	12	12
			30.6.81	0	1
Total no. of cases	50	50		50	50

Sampling

The research analysed data drawn from 399 cases: 200 cases were from referrals to the consultative committees, and 200 cases from the juvenile courts. In each section 100 cases (50 male, 50 female) were drawn from each location, so that overall the cases used consisted of a random sample stratified by sex and location.

Table 3.2   Sampling distribution

	Juvenile Courts		Consultative Panels		Total
	Town	City	Town	City	
No. of male cases	50	50	50	50	200
No. of female cases	49	50	50	50	199
Total	99	100	100	100	399

Table 3.2 shows the distribution of cases by location between courts and panels. One group of cases, that of female juvenile court cases in the town location, was not a random sample. Because the numbers of females appearing before the court in this small town was low (indeed many court sittings heard no female cases at all), then all female cases appearing before the court in this location were included in the sample. In order to complete the data collection within a reasonable time, it became necessary to include retrospectively some female cases from cases heard before the data collection began, as already indicated in Table 3.1a. One case proved not to be usable after completion of the data collection, and so the female sample for the town location was reduced to 49. Other cases from the juvenile court were selected randomly by the Clerk of the Court. Male cases were drawn as far as possible from the same court sittings.

Selection of the cases drawn from the referrals to the consultative committee was carried out randomly by the juvenile liaison sergeant, on a similar basis, aiming to include male and female cases from the same panel sitting. As in the case of the juvenile court in the town location, all female referrals were included, so that the female cases of both court and panels in this location included all female cases appearing before the panels and the courts during the period of this research.

The criteria used for selection in the court sample was that cases should be referred on criminal charges, not care proceedings. This was done to avoid the inevitable gender difference that would be apparent in the courts' protective, chivalrous role towards juvenile females considered to be 'exposed to moral danger' or 'beyond control of parent or guardian' (Children and Young Persons Act 1969, ss.1(c) and 1(d)). By comparing only cases brought under criminal proceedings, an obvious difference between males and females was removed, so enabling a more direct comparison between the two groups and providing a more rigorous test of any possible gender bias.

Data analysis

The data were coded by the researcher and a computer analysis undertaken using the SPSS programmes for cross-tabulation and for frequencies in general and condescriptive modes. In all cases where chi-square values are quoted, they have been corrected to two decimal places, and the figure quoted is always for the corrected chi-square values. The significance level chosen was 0.05.

Most of the coding undertaken did not involve subjective judgements on the part of the researcher, but one area which did so requires discussion. This is the comments made on each case by each participating agency, that is, police, social services, probation and education welfare, in the consultative panel meetings.

Comments made in the panel meetings were summarized on the data collection forms. These comments were processed for analysis in two ways, first, by a simple frequency count giving an indication of the amount of participation by each agency and the number of comments made under nine headings:

1 previous history;
2 family background;
3 educational ability;
4 school performance;
5 school attendance;
6 behaviour;
7 not known;
8 no comment;
9 other.

An assessment was then made by the researcher as to the nature of the comment which was coded into one of three categories: positive, negative and neutral.

A positive comment was judged to be one which might be supportive of the young person and seen to advocate leniency, for example:

'Very supportive parents. Has been chastized for this offence.' (Social Services)

'Lives with mother and siblings. Good girl at home. Regrets actions.' (Social Services)

'Admits. She is remorseful.' (Social Services)

'Home visited. Seems reasonably good.' (Social Services)

'Stated she had been encouraged to take part.' (Social Services)

'No problems. Polite, quiet, well-behaved.' (Social Services)

'No problem at school.' (Education Welfare)

'A capable and able pupil. Coping well.' (Education Welfare)

'Supportive parents, child easily led.' (Education Welfare)

'A lovable girl. Seeks love and attention. Shy, easily led. Mental age 8 years.' (Education Welfare)

'Previous good character.' (Police)

'First offender.' (Police)

   A negative comment was one which was judged to be derogatory and which might have an adverse influence on the panel's decision, for example:

'Parents separated. Financial problems. No recent involvement. Conditions in the home are grim.' (Social Services)

'A known glue-sniffer.' (Social Services)

'Parents divorced. Stepfather in prison for rape. Father also in prison.' (Social Services)

'Further offences committed since the one under consideration.' (Police)

'Previous conviction for dishonesty.' (Police)

'Family known. Two previous cautions.' (Police)

'Known. In care of local authority.' (Probation)

'Nuisance at times. Usually late for school.' (Education Welfare)

'Poor attendance. Parent not helpful.' (Education Welfare)

'Truculent. Mother suffers from depression.' (Education Welfare)

'Parents failed to attend school on request to discuss the matter.' (Education Welfare)

'Difficult boy. Often centre of disturbance at school.' (Education Welfare)

Occasionally stronger negative comments were noted, for example:

'Bad school attendance. Sly, devious, a nasty bit of work.' (Education Welfare)

'Nothing good. Malicious, dangerous, dull, ESN.' (Education Welfare)

'A nuisance and a villain.' (Education Welfare)

'Can be untrustworthy, underhanded, needs watching.' (Education Welfare)

'Family known. Home conditions shocking. Vast improvement lately.' (Social Services)

'Bad attendance, a dipsomaniac, Easily led, especially towards crime.' (Education Welfare)

Some comments were a combination of a positive comment in one of the categories and a negative comment in another, for example:

'No problem in school. Below average ability.'

This would have been coded as a positive value comment in category 6 (behaviour) and a negative value comment in category 3 (educational ability). And:

'Can be naughty and a troublemaker. Has ability but lazy.'

This would have been coded under three categories, thus: category 6 (behaviour) − negative; category 3 (educational ability) − positive; and category 4 (school performance) − negative.

Some comments were less easy to interpret, for example:

'Mixing with bad company. Behaviour satisfactory.'

On the assumption that this was quite an achievement for the young person involved, it was coded as positive under category 6 (behaviour).

A *neutral comment* was interpreted as one which simply gave information and appeared to be neither supportive nor derogatory, for example:

'Parents have just divorced.' (Education Welfare)

'Mother suffers with mental health.' (Social Services)

'Known. In care of local authority.' (Social Services)

'Previous involvement, nothing relevant.' (Social Services)

'Parents in middle of divorce proceedings.' (Probation)

Inevitably other interpretations than the one used for the coding could have been made on a number of the comments. For instance, 'Mother suffers with mental health' might have been interpreted as a negative comment. The positive, negative and neutral values placed on the agency comments were, therefore, to some extent subjective and dependent on the point of view of the researcher. However, all the comments were coded by the researcher to ensure a reasonable consistency in those judgements, and the majority of comments as can be seen from the positive and negative examples given, are clearly in one category or the other.

The present study has certain limitations: it took place in one police area; the numbers in the sample (399) are quite small and, therefore, any generalization of findings must be cautious; and data collection was restricted to the survey method from written agency records. However, it has also a number of features to commend it as a serious contribution in particular to the understanding of female juvenile delinquency. Its location in the UK is important. It will be apparent from the literature review in Chapter 2 that, with very few exceptions, most gender comparative studies have taken place in the USA. The direct gender comparison is an important feature, with an attempt being made as far as possible to include male and female cases from the same panel and court sittings. Many studies either exclude females altogether or compare two separate studies of males and females or incidentally report data on females to the main research findings. The present study is more comprehensive in scope than many other gender comparative studies, in that it controls for a wider range of variables which might affect the relationship between gender and the decision of the juvenile court. In an extensive literature search the researcher did not become aware of any similar study involving the consultative panels. This examination of possible gender bias at two levels in the justice system, as well as in two geographical locations, might be considered to add to the strength of the present study. Data collection was undertaken in the agencies by individuals closely involved with the cases: the Clerk of the Court, probation officers, social workers and juvenile liaison police sergeants, hence contributing to reliability of the data from first-hand knowledge of the cases. Coding and interpretation of the data were undertaken by the researcher, thus minimizing any inconsistency which might occur with more than one person being involved. Thus although having certain limitations, the present study has a number of strengths which contribute to confidence in the findings reported in the following chapters.

4 Gender and the consultative panels

This chapter reports and interprets the data obtained from a study of 100 male and 100 female cases considered by the police consultative panels in the research locations. The results of this section of the research are reported under the following headings:

1 Type of current offence and gender bias in panel recommendations.
2 Gender and the influence of value of current offence on panel recommendations.
3 Gender and the influence of previous history on panel recommendations.
4 Gender and the influence of age or current offence on panel recommendations.
5 Gender and agency comments in panel meetings.
6 Gender and stated reasons for panel recommendations.
7 Gender and location.

The figures summarizing the decisions made on the 200 cases considered by the two juvenile panels during the period of the research show that almost twice as many females as males receive a caution (Table 4.1), and so conversely, almost twice as many males are proceeded against.

The chi-square calculation indicates a highly significant result. The panel recommendation for all cases in the sample was divided roughly equally between the recommendations for caution and proceedings. No cases received a recommendation for no further action, although this is an option open to the panel. However, in only three cases the

Table 4.1   Sex, by panel recommendation

	Caution	Proceedings	Row Total
No. of males	36	64	100
No. of females	67	33	100
Total	103	97	200

$\chi^2 = 18.02$ 1 df $p < 0.001$

police superintendent did not accept the panel recommendation, and two of these three cases received a decision for no further action. The fact that no cases received a recommendation of no further action from the panel suggests an active policy by the police with the agreement of the welfare agencies in respect of juvenile delinquency. This is surprising in view of the fact that many of the cases included in the sample were first-time petty offenders (see Table 4.8) and might suggest that diversion was not a major function of the panels at the time of the research.

Nevertheless, whilst overall the panel recommendations may seem relatively harsh, it would appear that the panel is favourably disposed to females. These results correlate closely with the national figures, which show that police caution 46 per cent of all males aged 10 and under 17 found guilty or cautioned for indictable offences, whilst the comparable figures for females is 71 per cent (HMSO, 1981, pp.98−9).

Despite the highly significant difference in the figures for males and females in Table 4.1, it should not be assumed that this difference can be attributed to gender bias without further examination of the figures in the light of other variables which might affect the panel recommendation, such as: the nature of the offence charged, including type of offence and monetary value involved; the young person's previous history of offending, including number, type and value of previous offences; the age of the young person; and the nature of agency comments in the panel meetings which might influence the panel recommendation.

Type of current offence and gender bias in panel recommendations

It might be assumed that one reason for the panels' appearing to be more leniently disposed towards females is that the types of offence committed by females differ from the types of offence generally committed by males. In order to assess how influential the nature of the current offence was in relation to the panel recommendations and whether this was more influential than the gender factor, first, a summary of the offending patterns of males and females in the sample was established. Table 4.2a is a composite table identifying thirteen categories of offence and showing the numbers of offences in each category with which the young people in the sample were associated. Even though the sample consisted of 100 males and 100 females, the numbers add up to more than 100 in each sample because a small number of young people were associated with more than one current offence. Percentage figures have been corrected to one decimal point.

Table 4.2a Sex, by current offence

Category of offence		1	2	3	4	5	6	7	8	9	10	11	12	13	Total
Male	no.	3	1	15	1	20	22	0	14	1	2	3	5	21	108
	%	2.8	0.9	13.9	0.9	18.5	20.4	0	13.0	0.9	1.9	2.8	4.6	19.4	100
Female	no.	8	0	3	3	11	57	1	7	0	0	2	1	10	103
	%	7.8	0	2.9	2.9	10.7	55.3	1.0	6.8	0	0	1.9	1.0	9.7	100

Key:
1, violence against the person; 2, sexual offences; 3, burglary; 4, robbery; 5, theft and handling; 6, theft from store; 7, fraud and forgery; 8, criminal damage; 9, arson; 10, threatening behaviour; 11, offences involving consumption of alcohol; 12, theft of motor vehicle; 13, other.

Table 4.2b Sex, by current offence (grouped)

	Property offences	Offences against the person	Other	Total
	(Categories 3, 4, 5, 6, 7, 8, 9, 12)	(Categories 1, 2, 10)	(Categories 11, 13)	
Percentage of males committing offences	72.2	5.6	22.2	100
Percentage of females committing offences	80.6	7.8	11.6	100

Although there are differences observable from the table in the numbers of offences committed by males and females in some categories, the only two categories of offence where the difference is statistically significant are: category 3 (burglary) $\chi^2 = 7.38705$; 1 df; $p < 0.01$, and category 6 (theft from store) $\chi^2 = 24.18660$; 1 df; $p < 0.001$. The high proportion of female shoplifters stands out clearly in this grouping and is at odds with data from self-report studies discussed earlier, where males and females admit to more similar patterns of offending. It may be that gender bias operates at a very early stage in the process, with store detectives being more alert for females; it may be that males commit shoplifting offences along with other offences, and those offences being seen as the more serious becoming the ones which are charged, the shoplifting offences being grouped under offences taken into consideration and therefore not categorized; or of course it may be that shoplifting is a predominant feature of female delinquency. Further research is needed on gender bias prior to police cautioning and on the comparison of male and female delinquency patterns. Despite this very significant difference in the category, a crude re-grouping of offences to distinguish between property offences and offences against the person indicates no significant difference between male and female sub-samples (Table 4.2b). Offences against the person would generally be considered as serious offences. The lack of significant gender difference indicates that this factor cannot be used to suggest that males are committing more serious offences. Further analysis of the property offence grouping is carried out in the following section.

These figures from the two locations in which the research was carried out reflect closely the national figures for England and Wales. Table 4.3 shows the national figures in a similar, though not exactly corresponding, breakdown of offences in groups to those in Table 4.2b, but the correspondence of the figures in the two tables is clear.

In order to test the interrelationships between types of offence committed by the young people in the sample, gender and panel recommendation, cross-tabulations of sex by panel recommendation controlling for category of offence were carried out. Table 4.4 is a composite table summarizing those cross-tabulations; it records the number of male and female offenders in each category who were recommended to receive cautions or against whom proceedings were recommended. Category 13 has been omitted from this table as it is a composite category made up of a number of differing offences and thus rendering male—female comparisons inapplicable.

As can be seen from Table 4.4, the number of cases represented in each category is very small and it is, therefore, inappropriate to draw hard-and-fast conclusions from this data. What is clear, however, is an

Table 4.3 National figures (England and Wales) for types of offence for which juveniles were cautioned or found guilty, 1979

| | Boys | | Girls | | All juveniles |
	14—16 (%)	10—13 (%)	14—16 (%)	10—13 (%)	(%)
Theft	60	68	83	91	67
Burglary	23	23	6	5	20
Violence against the person	8	3	7	2	6
Criminal damage	3	4	1	1	3
All other offences	6	2	3	1	4

Note: 'Theft predominates with the girls; burglary and criminal damage are 3 or 4 times more prevalent among boys. Violence against the person, though, varies more with age than sex' (DHSS, 1981, p.20).

observable trend in categories 3, 4, 5, 6 and 8 for the panel recommendation to be harsher for males than for females. In each of those categories proportionately more females than males were recommended for cautioning. It follows that conversely in each of these categories fewer females were recommended for court proceedings than males. An exception to this trend is in the figures for category 1, where seven out of eight females were recommended for proceedings, whereas two out of three males received a caution. Whilst care in interpreting these figures is required, because of the small numbers involved, it is possible that the results for category 1 offences reflect societal values on gender-role differences where violence is seen to be less inappropriate in the male role than in the female role. In two categories of offences, 11 and 12, both males and females received similar treatment.

Tentative conclusions from these data would appear to be that where offences are comparable, the panels seem to treat females more leniently on the whole, with the exception of offences involving violence against the person where females appeared to have been treated more harshly in the sample. In addition to controlling for type of offence, another means of assessing the seriousness of the offence(s) charged is to compare the value ascribed to the offence where property offences have been committed.

Table 4.4 Sex, by panel recommendation controlling for offence by category

Category of offence		Panel recommendation	
		Caution no.	Proceedings no.
1 Violence against the person	M	2	1
	F	1	7
2 Sexual offences	M	1	–
	F	–	–
3 Burglary	M	2	13
	F	1	2
4 Robbery	M	–	1
	F	3	–
5 Theft and handling	M	4	16
	F	6	5
6 Theft from store	M	15	7
	F	46	11
7 Fraud and forgery	M	–	–
	F	1	–
8 Criminal damage	M	2	12
	F	2	5
9 Arson	M	–	1
	F	–	–
10 Threatening behaviour	M	–	2
	F	–	–
11 Offences involving consumption of alcohol	M	3	–
	F	2	–
12 Theft of motor vehicle	M	5	–
	F	1	–

Gender and the influence of value of current offence on panel recommendations

It could be argued perhaps in the case of property offences, which constitute the majority of offences committed by juveniles (Tables 4.2b and 4.3), that girls commit fewer serious offences and that this would therefore influence the panel's recommendation, making it appear more leniently disposed towards girls when in fact seriousness of offence would be a more important factor than gender.

Table 4.5a cross-tabulates sex by total value ascribed to the current offence. It shows that most young people in the sample are petty offenders: 71 per cent of males and 86 per cent of females in the sample have offences where the monetary value involved was assessed at less than £25. If overall the picture is of petty offenders, a comparison of males and females shows a highly significant association between sex and the value of the offence. More girls appear in the £1—£25 categories than boys, and therefore more boys appear in the higher-value categories. Table 4.5b shows the breakdown for the higher-value category.

Table 4.5a   Sex, by total value of current offence

	No value		£5 and under		£6—£25		£25—£100		£100 and over		Total	
	no.	(%)	no.	(%)	no.	(%)	no.	(%)	no.	(%)	no.	(%)
Male	32	36.4	25	28.4	14	15.9	7	8.0	10	11.4	88	48.6
Female	21	22.6	29	31.2	36	38.7	5	5.4	2	2.2	93	51.4

χ^2 = 17.80   4 df p < 0.01

Note: 19 missing observations

Table 4.5b   High-values breakdown: sex, by current offence

	Value ascribed to current offence (£s)								
No. of cases	109	120	131	150	157	168	225	400	900
Male	1	2	1	1	1	0	2	1	1
Female	0	0	0	0	0	1	0	0	1

Having established that there appears to be a significant difference in the value ascribed to the offences committed by males and females, how far the monetary value involved in the offence influences the panel recommendation can be seen from the cross-tabulation of sex by panel recommendation controlling for value of current offence. Tables 4.6a and b show that the highly significant association between sex and panel recommendation observed in Table 4.1 now disappears, suggesting that the value of the offence has some influence. For the two higher-value categories (£26–£100 and over £100) where the numbers involved are small, Fisher's exact test (2-tailed) showed no significance.

Table 4.6a Sex, by panel recommendation controlling for offences value £5 and under

	Caution		Proceedings		Total	
	no.	(%)	no.	(%)	no.	(%)
Male	13	52	12	48	25	46.3
Female	23	79.3	6	20.7	29	53.7

$\chi^2 = 3.36$ 1 df   p = n.s.

Table 4.6b Sex, by panel recommendation controlling for offences value £6–£25

	Caution		Proceedings		Total	
	no.	(%)	no.	(%)	no.	(%)
Male	8	57.1	6	42.9	14	28.0
Female	31	86.1	5	13.9	36	72.0

$\chi^2 = 3.39$ 1 df   p = n.s.

As shown in Tables 4.6a and b, although the association is marginally not significant, there does appear to be a trend for more females to be cautioned than males in the lower-value categories. On the higher-value categories no females, but two males, received cautions. One must conclude from the statistical analysis that the value of the offence overrides the importance of gender, but also that this is an area warranting further research.

Gender and the influence of previous history on panel recommendations

Table 4.7 shows that significantly more females than males whose cases were considered by the panels were first-time offenders: 86 per cent of the female sample and 68 per cent of the male sample being first offenders, giving an average percentage over the whole sample of 77 per cent first offenders. No offenders in the sample have more than three previous offences, although three males in the sample had respectively five, seven and nine previous offences taken into consideration. This information, together with the data on the type of current offence and the monetary values associated, builds up a picture of the young people whose cases are brought to the juvenile panels as predominantly first-time petty offenders.

Table 4.7   Sex, by number of previous offences

| | Number of previous offences | | | | |
	0	1	2	3	Total
Male	68	23	8	1	100
Female	86	10	3	1	100
Total	154	33	11	2	200
Percentage of total sample	77.0	16.5	5.5	1.0	

$\chi^2 = 9.50$ 3 df $p < 0.05$

In order to assess how far the previous history of the young person influenced the panel recommendation, cross-tabulations of sex by panel recommendation controlling for numbers of previous offences were obtained. Table 4.8 shows that the greater number of cautions received by females over the whole sample (Table 4.1) is still significant when first offenders are selected out.

If the cross-tabulation is repeated controlling for those cases with one previous offence recorded, then it becomes clear that this is a significant factor influencing the panel recommendation: no cases with one previous offence were cautioned. All, irrespective of gender, received a recommendation for proceedings. Since 100 per cent of both females and males with one previous offence were all recommended for proceedings, it can be assumed that the existence of a previous offence on record is stronger than the gender factor. An examination of the data relating to cases with two and three previous offences shows that all cases irrespective of gender were recommended for proceedings. However, the numbers involved are too small in these categories to draw statistical significance (eight males and three females had two previous offences, and one male and one female had three previous offences).

Table 4.8   Sex, by panel recommendation: first offenders

		Caution	Proceedings	Total
Male	no.	36	32	68
	%	52.9	47.1	44.2
Female	no.	67	19	86
	%	7.7.9	22.1	55.8

$\chi^2 = 9.59$ 1 df   p <0.01

Note: Percentage figures refer to percentage of first-time offenders.

Type of previous offence

As indicated (see Table 4.8), the majority (77 per cent) of young people in the sample were first-time offenders. The number of previous offences committed in all of the thirteen categories was therefore very small — too small to be able to draw conclusions from cross-tabulating sex by panel recommendation by category of previous offence. As might be expected, the pattern of offending for the previous offences was similar to the pattern of offending for current offences; Table 4.9 gives a comparison of those patterns.

It is clear from Table 4.8 that possession of a record involving a previous offence is a most significant factor in influencing the panel recommendation, and since all cases with one or more previous offences received recommendations for proceedings, then clearly the existence of previous offences is the significant factor rather than the nature of the previous offences as represented by the category or monetary value associated with the offence. This view is supported by the figures representing reasons for the panel recommendation. In 43 cases a previous conviction or caution was given as the reason for the panel recommendation. This represents a high proportion of the sample which had previous offences recorded (i.e. 46).

Table 4.9 Comparison of number of previous offences and current offences committed in each category

Category of offence	Previous offence		Current offence	
	Male	Female	Male	Female
1 Violence against the person	2	0	3	8
2 Sexual offences	0	0	1	0
3 Burglary	11	2	15	3
4 Robbery	0	0	1	3
5 Thefts and handling	8	5	20	11
6 Theft from store	5	5	22	57
7 Fraud and forgery	0	1	0	1
8 Criminal damage	6	1	14	7
9 Arson	0	0	1	0
10 Threatening behaviour	0	0	2	0
11 Offences involving consumption of alcohol	1	0	3	2
12 Theft of motor vehicle	1	0	5	1
13 Other	6	3	16	10

Gender and the influence of age or current offence on panel recommendations

Table 4.10 illustrates the figures for the mean age of all offenders in the sample (column 1), also for first offenders only (column 2) and for those with previous offences (column 3).

Table 4.10 Sex, by age

			Years/months	
		All	First offenders	Recidivists
Male	Mean	14.8	14.8	14.8
	Min.	10.6	10.7	10.7
	Max.	16.9	16.9	16.8
	Range	6.3	6.3	6.2
Female	Mean	14.4	14.2	15.5
	Min.	10.3	10.3	12.9
	Max.	17.0	17.0	16.8
	Range	6.7	6.7	3.8

No obvious difference between the male and female sample is apparent, the few months difference in the mean age is probably accounted for by the higher number of first offenders in the female sample. The chi-square figure obtained in a cross-tabulation of sex by age groups (Table 4.11), however, confirms a significant association between gender and age in the total sample: more females fall into the younger age-groups than males, although overall the majority (67 per cent) of the young people came into the 14—17 age-group.

Table 4.11   Sex, by age-group

	10—13		14—17		Row total	
	no.	%	no.	%	no.	%
Male	24	24.0	76	76.0	100	50.0
Female	42	42.0	58	58.0	100	50.0
					200	100.0

$\chi^2 = 6.54$ 1 df $p < 0.02$

Evidence from studies on police cautioning suggests that age is a significant factor in the decision to caution. Goldman's (1963) study shows that in the age-group 9—13 the court referral rate is approximately 30 per cent, and from age 14 upwards increases steeply to just under 50 per cent for 17-year-olds. The results of this American study are comparable in the UK with the findings of Priestley, Fears and Fuller (1977). Figure 4.1 illustrates their findings in two police areas in Britain. These findings for males only suggest a direct relationship between age and the possibility of court proceedings. Although percentages vary in each police area, the clear overall trend is for older boys to be prosecuted and younger boys to receive cautions. Too few girls were included in this sample, they report, for the figures to be as reliable, but it appeared that a broadly similar pattern applies to the female group. National patterns based on the *Criminal Statistics (England and Wales)* for 1979 are not directly comparable as they include only indictable offences; nevertheless, as Figure 4.2 shows, a broadly similar pattern is apparent. Whilst this graph shows broad trends over more than a decade, the position of the age-groups represented shows that the highest percentage of cautions is received by girls in the younger age-group and the lowest percentage of cautions by boys in the older age-group.

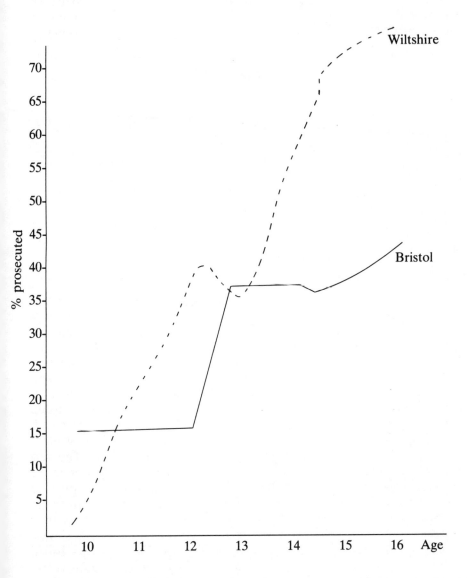

Source: Priestley, Fears and Fuller, 1977, p.66.

Figure 4.1   Children prosecuted in Wiltshire and Bristol

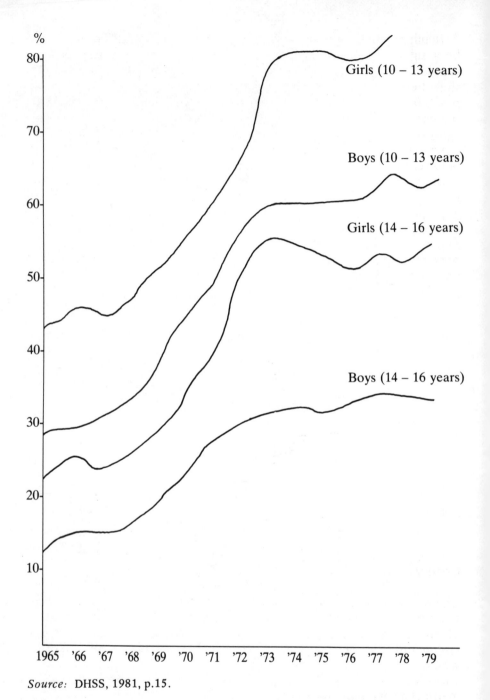

%
80–
70–
60–
50–
40–
30–
20–
10–

Girls (10 – 13 years)

Boys (10 – 13 years)

Girls (14 – 16 years)

Boys (14 – 16 years)

1965 '66 '67 '68 '69 '70 '71 '72 '73 '74 '75 '76 '77 '78 '79

Source: DHSS, 1981, p.15.

Figure 4.2 Cautioning rate for juvenile offenders found guilty of, or cautioned for, indictable offences 1965–79

It might, therefore, be expected in the present study that age would be a significant factor in influencing the panel recommendation, and indeed Table 4.12 confirms this, showing a highly significant relationship between age and panel recommendation (χ^2 = 14.17; 1 df; p < 0.001). In fact 71.2 per cent of the 10–13 age-group received a recommendation for caution, whilst only 41.8 per cent of the older age-group received the same recommendation. However, when these figures are broken down by gender, there is no significant relationship between age-group and panel recommendation for males (χ^2 = 1.95; 1 df; p = n.s.), but the relationship between age-group and panel recommendation for females is significant (χ^2 = 7.51; 1 df; p < 0.01). This probably reflects the larger number of males in the older age-groups, and the larger number of younger females. To decide how much of the advantage is given to females because of their gender and how much because of their age is not possible from the present data, but clearly both age and gender are highly significant in relation to panel recommendation.

Table 4.12   Sex, by age by panel recommendation

	Caution		Proceedings	
	no.	%	no.	%
Male:				
10–13	12	33.3	12	18.7
14–17	24	66.7	52	81.2
Female:				
10–13	35	52.2	7	21.2
14–17	32	47.8	26	78.8

Gender and agency comments in panel meetings

Agency participation in the panel meetings was assessed on the basis of the frequency and nature of the comments made by the representatives of the participating agencies. Table 4.13 shows total figures for all comments made by agencies in the panel, excluding those categories which recorded 'no comment' and 'not known'. No significant difference is observed in the frequency of agencies' comments overall on males and females.

Table 4.14 gives a breakdown into nine categories of the figures

Table 4.13   Sex, by number of cases on which agencies commented

	Police		Probation		Social services		Education welfare		Row total
	no.	%	no.	%	no.	%	no.	%	
Male	57	54.8	16	50.0	51	53.7	159	48.5	283 50.6%
Female	47	45.2	16	50.0	44	46.3	169	51.5	276 49.4%

summarized in Table 4.13 for the participation of the agencies in the consultative panel. The distribution of comments is much as one might expect, and it seems clear that agencies operate on the lines of clear role boundaries within the panels. Police comment mostly on previous history; probation comment on previous history and family background; social services comment on previous history and also family background, and occasionally on behaviour; and education welfare comment on a range including school and background information, though with an emphasis on the two categories school attendance and behaviour. The table shows that the most active agency was the Education Welfare Department, whose comments totalled 58.2 per cent of all the comments made. To some extent, this might be accounted for by the fact that the local education authority is the only agency of the four represented which comes into contact with all young people and, therefore, the Education Welfare Department has access to this information. It seems clear also from the low participation of probation that agencies comment only on cases known to them, so do not see their role as 'consultative' in the sense that they represent a professional viewpoint which may have a different focus than that of other agencies, and therefore may have something to contribute on issues of principle even where cases are not known to them. An examination of the table with regard to evidence of gender bias suggests that there are two categories where the chi-square calculation is significant: police comments on previous history, and education welfare comments on behaviour.

It is interesting to note that a comparison of the *frequency* of police comments with regard to the previous history of males and females is not significant (χ^2 = 0.98; 1 df; p = n.s.), whilst a comparison of the nature of the comments does show a gender difference (χ^2 = 21.54; 3 df; p < 0.001, see Table 4.14), the police being twice as likely to

Table 4.14 Breakdown of number of cases commented on and nature of agency comments in panels

No. of comments		Police			Probation			Social services			Education welfare		
		Positive	Negative	Neutral	Positive	Negative	Neutral	Positive	Negative	Neutral	Positive	Negative	Neutral
1* Previous history	Male	16	15	25	0	1	8	1	7	14	1	1	2
	Female	32	12	4	0	3	8	0	6	7	0	1	1
2 Family background	Male		nil		0	2	2	3	4	7	2	9	3
	Female				1	4	3	3	9	2	2	8	0
3 Educational ability	Male		nil			nil			nil		3	9	7
	Female										1	7	3
4 School performance	Male		nil			nil			nil		2	3	0
	Female										1	1	0
5 School attendance	Male		nil			nil			nil		14	20	1
	Female										21	17	3
6 Behaviour	Male		nil			nil		0	1	0	23	32	4
	Female							1	1	0	46	26+	2
7 Not known	Male		n.a.			n.a.			n.a.			n.a.	
	Female												
8 No comment	Male		n.a.			n.a.			n.a.			n.a.	
	Female												
9 Other	Male	0	1	0	2	0	0	3	2	5	10	14	3
	Female	1	0	0	2	0	0	6	6	4	9	17	12
Totals		49	28	29	5	10	21	17	36	39	134	165	27

* $\chi^2 = 21.54$ 3 df $p < 0.001$

+ $\chi^2 = 13.38$ 3 df $p < 0.01$

comment positively on a female than on a male and much less likely to be neutral in the case of a female. Only 4 neutral comments were recorded on female cases against 25 neutral comments for male cases. However, caution should be exercised in interpreting this as gender bias because of the significantly larger numbers of first-time offenders amongst the female sub-sample.

An interesting feature also emerges when the police comments on previous history are set against the figures for cases with previous offences recorded (see Table 4.7). Table 4.15 shows the number of cases where police comments on previous history and the number of cases with previous offences are recorded. The third column shows that for both males and females there is a discrepancy between these numbers, but that the discrepancy is greater for females.

Table 4.15   Sex, by number of cases known to police

	No. of cases where police comment on previous history	No. of cases with previous offences recorded	Difference
Male	56	32	24
Female	48	14	34

Without further substantiating evidence, conclusions drawn must inevitably be cautious, but it might appear that the cases in the difference column are cases known informally to the police through local knowledge. It shows that there were more females than males, and it might be assumed that the existence of a larger group of female juveniles known informally to the police implies that the police may be more reluctant to take action where females are concerned, and that they tend to be screened out of the system prior to the consultative panel stage. This points to an interesting area for further research. Studies of cautioning (e.g. Steer, 1970; Ditchfield, 1976; Priestley, Fears and Fuller, 1977; Landau, 1981) have not included significant discussion of female juveniles.

The second category showing a significant association between agency comments and gender (Table 4.14) is the comments on behaviour of the Education Welfare Department. Table 4.16 shows that 66.7 per cent of the positive comments made by this agency are made about females, whereas only 33.3 per cent were made about males. Of negative comments made, 44.8 per cent are made about

Table 4.16 Sex, by nature of education welfare comments on behaviour

	No comment		Positive comment		Negative comment		Neutral comment		Row total
	no.	%	no.	%	no.	%	no.	%	
Male	41	63.1	23	33.3	32	55.2	4	66.7	100 50.5%
Female	24	36.9	46	66.7	26	44.8	2	33.3	98 (2 missing observations) 49.5%
	65	32.8	69	34.8	58	29.3	6	3.0	198 100%

$\chi^2 = 13.38$ 3 df p < 0.001

females, whilst 55.2 per cent are made about males. Whereas it was not possible to assume gender bias in the police comments because they referred to previous history, and the existence of more female first-offenders in the sample would naturally effect this, in the present instance there can be no such qualification, and it appears that girls' behaviour is commented upon more favourably than boys in the sample.

Influence on panel recommendation

In order to test out whether these two categories (i.e. police comments on previous history and education welfare comments on behaviour) had any influence on the panel recommendation, 2 X 2 tables were prepared comparing sex by panel recommendation and controlling for each of these variables. In each case the tables clearly reflect the trend observed in Table 4.1 for significantly more females to be cautioned than males. A similar exercise controlling for negative comments by these agencies in the categories mentioned showed that negative comments by the police in all cases were consistent with a recommendation for court proceedings. However, the important factor here is the possession of a prior record as a policy factor for recommending proceedings. A comparison of sex by panel recommendation controlling for negative comments by education welfare still shows a significant gender difference in the recommendations for caution in favour of females ($\chi^2 = 7.81$; 1 df; p < 0.01), suggesting that the overall gender bias in favour of females is not affected by the agency's negative comments in this area. Where figures permitted (see Table 4.14), similar values were obtained for other agencies and other categories despite the fact that these were not shown to be significant in Table 4.14. Nothing of significant interest can be reported from these and the conclusion is that generally other factors were more important in the panel's reaching their recommendation than agency comments in these categories. It implies that policy decisions, for instance, age, seriousness of offence and possession of a prior record, are more important. A larger-scale survey with large numbers may have brought out the fact that in cases where there are known extenuating circumstances, then agency comments may have had more influence. The most that can be said of the function of agency comments in the panel is that the panel operates as a monitoring device, and presumably operates as a safety net to avoid harsh, unjust action where very adverse circumstances operate. However, the low level of participation in those categories covering family background (Table 4.14) would suggest that this safety net has rather large holes, and gives little confidence in this aspect of the panels' operation.

The conclusions that can justifiably be drawn from an examination of the comments and frequency of participation of the social work agencies is that they do not in any respect act as advocates for the young people. Both social services and probation made twice as many negative comments as positive ones about the young people. The idea that social workers represent a 'soft' approach to juvenile offenders is not, therefore, borne out in the analysis of cases in this sample.

If the stereotype of the 'soft' social worker is not borne out, nor is the stereotype of the 'hard' approach of the police. These popular stereotypes probably derive from the conflict within the juvenile justice system of a welfare and a justice approach, and the association of a welfare approach with the social work agencies and a justice approach with the police.

Only just over a quarter of police comments were negative, and they are the agency with the highest percentage of positive comments. Some caution needs to be exercised in the interpretation of these figures, however, as 'previous good character' would be noted as a positive comment and therefore the number of positive comments would be directly influenced by the large number of first offenders in the sample. This reservation is, however, balanced by the number of neutral comments made by the police, which is roughly equal to the number of negative comments. The overall impression is of a fairly positive attitude on the part of the police to the young people and a more negative approach by the social work agencies.

Gender and stated reasons for panel recommendations

If the agency comments within the meeting appear to have little influence on the panel decision, then the assumption is that previously agreed policies are an overriding influence. Table 4.17 examines reasons given for panel decisions, prior coding of this section having been related to the current policy for decision-making in the panels. It can be seen that gender differences are highly significant. The most outstanding gender difference in the table is the large number of females pleading guilty. This may be an interesting example of gender-role expectation, in that greater expectation is placed on females to conform to authority. The gender differences reported in columns 2 and 4 are expected, reflecting differences reported elsewhere in this report. However, the larger numbers of females admitting guilt also accounts, to some extent, for the greater number of cautions received by females, since admission of guilt is a prerequisite factor for cautioning, and the number of female admissions of guilt and the number of females cautioned in the sample is the same (N = 67). In order to fully analyse gender bias, further research involving interviews with females who admit guilt is indicated in order to understand better the factors leading to their admission, and also comparison with a sample of males.

Table 4.17 Sex, by reason for panel recommendation

		Guilty plea	Previous conviction	Previous caution	Seriousness of offence	Claim pending	Local policy	Other	Row total
		1	2	3	4	5	6	7	
Male	no.	34	19	9	13	2	1	22	100
	%	33.7	73.1	52.9	68.4	50.0	100	11.0	50%
Female	no.	67	7	8	6	2	0	10	100
	%	66.3	26.9	47.1	31.6	50.0	0	31.2	50%

χ^2 = 24.63   7 df   p < 0.001

Gender and location

An interesting gender bias emerges in a comparison of panel recommendations in location A and location B according to sex. It can be seen from Table 4.18 that in city location A a highly significant relationship (χ^2 = 20.34; 1 df; p < 0.001) is observable between sex and panel recommendation, reflecting the difference in the overall sample (see Table 4.1). However, in location B (town) there is no such significant gender bias observable (χ^2 = 2.01; 1 df; p = n.s.). In order to explore the possible reasons for this, the numbers of cases with a previous history of offending was examined in each location since this variable was found to be significant in the general sample. Table 4.19 shows previous offending patterns, and it can be observed that in town location B there is a small group of both male and female recidivists.

Table 4.18   Gender, panel recommendation and location

	Caution		Proceedings	
	no.	%	no.	%
Male				
Location A (city)	19	31.1	31	79.5
Location B (town)	17	40.5	33	56.9
Female				
Location A (city)	42	68.9	8	20.5
Location B (town)	25	59.5	25	43.1

Note: Percentages refer to percentage of cautions or proceedings in each location.

Table 4.19   Sex, by place by number of previous offences

		No. of previous offences				
		0	1	2	3	Total
City location A	Males	32	17	1	0	50
	Females	48	2	0	0	50
Town location B	Males	36	6	7	1	50
	Females	38	8	3	1	50

With the exception of females in location A, where the numbers are higher, the numbers of first offenders are fairly evenly distributed. A larger number of males with one previous offence is apparent in location A, but the incidence of offending then drops more rapidly than in location B where a small group of males continues to offend again. Overall there is apparent a greater gender difference in incidence of offending in the city than in the town where a small group of females, like the males, continues to offend. This very small group of recidivists in the town location B is likely to account for some of the location difference in panel recommendation, and as the pattern of male and female recidivism is similar in the town and the city this variable clearly overrides gender bias in the town.

Frequency counts of the number of cases on which agencies comment show that the police are considerably more active in town location B (Table 4.20). It can be seen that they make more positive comments on the previous history of females (twice as many as on males) in town location B. Police in city location A make no positive comments, and their comments there are mostly neutral. It may be that the greater police activity in town location B also contributes to the differences between the two locations in panel recommendations.

Table 4.20 Frequency of police comments in category 1, by location

| | City location A | | | Town location B | | |
	Positive	Negative	Neutral	Positive	Negative	Neutral
Male	0	1	17	16	14	8
Female	0	0	1	32	12	3
Totals	0	1	18	48	26	11

A similar frequency count for social services' comments in three categories: 1 (previous history), 2 (family background) and 9 (other), shows that although the differences are not statistically significant, social services appear to be slightly more active in the town location than in the city and that their participation in the town consists of more negative comments (Table 4.21).

Frequency counts for probation activity produced very small numbers, but again show more total participation and more negative participation in the town location than in the city. The figures for education welfare, unlike the other agencies, showed remarkably little difference between the locations (Table 4.22).

Table 4.21   Frequency of social services' comments in categories 1, 2 and 9, by location

	City location A			Town location B		
	Positive	Negative	Neutral	Positive	Negative	Neutral
Male	2	0	9	5	13	17
Female	0	3	3	9	12	10
Totals	2	3	12	14	25	27

Table 4.22   Frequency of education welfare comments in categories 1, 2, 3, 4, 5, 6 and 9, by location

	City location A			Town location B		
	Positive	Negative	Neutral	Positive	Negative	Neutral
Male	27	36	6	28	42	10
Female	42	36	5	38	41	6
Totals	69	72	11	66	83	16

The overall pattern of agency comments on cases is that with the exception of education welfare there is a trend for the agencies to be more active in the town. Clearly, with a smaller population and smaller geographical area, the young people can be more easily identified. This appears to operate against the interests of females, who do not receive the same gender bias as city and national figures reflect.

Comparison of offences in town and city

Location differences were indicated in Table 4.19, but there were no significant gender differences in the pattern of previous offending. Similarly, a comparison of the type of current offence committed by the young people in the study showed no significant gender differences in the locations, with the exception of one category of offence, namely shoplifting. As might be expected, in the city where a number of large stores create greater opportunities for shoplifting, the rate for both males and females is higher than in the town: 76 per cent of the city female sample and 38 per cent of the town female sample were being considered for shoplifting offences. The figures for males were 30 per cent of the city sample and 14 per cent of the town sample. However, there was no significant difference to be found in a comparison of gender, location and total values ascribed to current offence.

It seems clear from this section of the study that there is no evidence to suggest that female delinquency is more serious in the city. Indeed, using recidivism as evidence of seriousness, the data suggest that female delinquency is in fact more serious in the town than in the city.

Summary

Overall it was clear that while approximately half the cases considered by the panels were recommended for cautioning and approximately half were recommended for court proceedings, significantly more females than males were cautioned. In order to explore the reason for this apparent gender bias, cross-tabulations of gender by panel recommendations were carried out controlling for a number of variables: type of offence; value ascribed to current offence; previous offending record; age; the nature and frequency of the comments of participating agencies; stated reason for panel recommendation; and location differences between town and city.

It was found that the gender difference in panel recommendations could not be clearly accounted for by differences in the types of offence committed by males and females. There is some indication that where offences are comparable, then females are treated more leniently, with the exception of offences involving violence against the person, where females not only lose the advantage of leniency which they are given in other offence categories, but are treated more harshly than males in this category. There is some evidence that the value ascribed to an offence becomes important over £25.

Previous offence record was found to be more important than gender in influencing panel recommendations.

Regarding age, it appeared that the younger age-group were more leniently treated in the case of females but that age was not significant in the male sub-sample. This finding differs from national figures and is probably explained to some extent by more younger females and more older males in the overall sample.

Agency participation in the panel meetings was measured by the number of cases on which agencies commented, and also by coding their comments into positive, negative and neutral categories. No significant gender difference was observed in the frequency of agency comments on cases. However, it was observed that the police comment on previous history more positively and more often on females than males, though this obviously is influenced by the larger number of first-time offenders in the female sub-sample, so cannot necessarily be ascribed to gender bias. An interesting factor emerged from the analysis of police comments in this area, in that there appears to be a group of juveniles known informally to the police and that there were more girls than boys represented, suggesting that gender bias may be operating at an earlier stage and girls are thus being screened out at a stage prior to the consultation panel. Education welfare commented more favourably on girls' behaviour than on boys'. It appeared that overall agency comments in the panel affect the panel recommendation less than previously agreed factors such as previous history, age and seriousness of offence. The low level of participation of agencies covering areas other than previous history, behaviour and school performance suggest little confidence in any monitoring function which the panel may take on.

An interesting feature was the large numbers of females pleading guilty. It may be that some gender bias operates in this area, in that it reflects the greater societal expectation of the female gender role to conform to authority. It is also clearly linked with the large number of female cautions in the sample since a guilty plea is a prerequisite factor for cautioning a young offender.

With regard to panel recommendation and location, an interesting gender difference emerges between town and city since there appears to be no significant gender bias in the recommendations of the town's panel. An examination of offending patterns suggested that this is closely linked with previous offending record and that this, in turn, reflects a greater frequency of cases on which agencies, except education welfare, comment in the town. Female offending is not more serious in the city, though significantly more females were charged with shoplifting in that location. If measured by recidivism then there was evidence from the data to suggest that female delinquency is more serious in the town location.

An interesting factor which emerged from the research, though not related directly to gender bias, was the roles played by the participating agencies. The population conception of a 'hard' police approach to juvenile crime and a 'soft' social work approach is not borne out. Social workers and probation officers made twice as many negative as positive comments on the young people. The percentage of police comments which were negative was the lowest figure for any agency and the percentage of positive police comments was the highest for any agency.

Agencies tended to comment specifically on cases known to them rather than generally on issues of principle from their own professional viewpoint. Comments made by agencies were largely as might be expected: police commented on previous history; social services on previous history and family background, occasionally on behaviour; probation commented on previous history and family background; and education welfare comments were found in all categories but were focused particularly on school attendance and behaviour.

There appeared to be little sense of the welfare agencies acting as advocates for the young people, or as consultants to the police except in cases known to them.

A further interesting feature emerging from these data with regard to policy on juvenile crime is that all cases considered by the panel received a recommendation for action, either caution or proceedings. No cases were recommended by the panels for no further action, although this is an option open to them. This is despite the fact that many of the juveniles in the sample were young, petty first-time offenders, suggesting a rather harsh response to juvenile offending in the two locations under consideration, and no active policy of diversion of young offenders from the juvenile justice system at the time of the research.

5 Gender and the juvenile courts

This chapter reports and interprets the data from the second phase of the research designed to examine the nature of gender bias, if any, operating in the decisions made about juveniles appearing before two juvenile courts on criminal charges. As reported previously, one of these courts was in city location A, the other in town location B; 199 cases were examined in this section of the research, 100 male cases and 99 female cases.

The data are reported in three sections: (1) gender and court disposals; (2) gender differences in family structure and socio-economic status; and (3) location differences and female offending.

I Gender and court disposals

A comparison of the main disposal by gender for each case showed unexpectedly, and in contrast to the decisions made by the consultative panels, that there appeared to be no statistically significant gender bias operating at this stage of the legal process.

Table 5.1a shows the numbers and percentages for each disposal available to the court. Since the numbers in several of the categories were very small, this table was collapsed into three main categories; this also had the advantage of excluding attendance centre and detention centre categories which are not directly comparable on a gender basis. The chi-square test when applied (Table 5.1b) showed no significance at the 0.05 level. It should be noted, however, that Table 5.1a shows

Table 5.1a Sex, by court disposals

		Bound over	Conditional discharge	Fine	Attendance centre	Supervision Order (probation)	Supervision Order (social services)	Supervision Order + IT to Probation	Supervision Order + IT to SSD	Deferred sentence	Detention Centre	Care Order	Crown Court, Borstal recall	Other	Row total
Male	no.	2	32	25	5	15	1	4	0	3	7	4	2	0	100
	%	1.0	16.1	12.6	2.5	7.5	0.5	2.0	0	1.5	3.5	2.0	1.0	0	
Female	no.	0	46	15	0	18	9	1	1	2	0	3	0	4	99
	%	0	23.1	7.5	0	9.0	4.5	0.5	0.5	1.0	0	1.5	0	2.0	

Table 5.1b Sex, by court disposals (grouped)

		Conditional discharge	Fine	All Supervision Orders	Row total
Male	no.	32	25	20	77
Female	no.	46	15	29	90

$\chi^2 = 5.69$ 2 df   p = n.s.

that 7 per cent more females than males received a conditional discharge, and although Table 5.1b shows this and other differences to be not significant, the significance figure was marginal. Probability tables for the distribution of χ^2 indicate that significance at the 0.05 level with two degrees of freedom occurs at 5.99 and the chi-square figure reported is 5.69 (Table 5.1b).

In 73 of the cases second disposals were indicated, and usually consisted of fines or other form of compensation in addition to the main disposal resulting from the offences charged. Table 5.2 shows that there was a significant difference, in that males were more often fined than females in addition to the main disposition and, therefore, this might be interpreted as an indication that the courts treat males more harshly.

Table 5.2   Sex, by further court disposals

		Fines	Other	Row total
Male	no.	13	28	41
	%	17.6	37.8	56.8
Female	no.	3	29	32
	%	4.1	39.2	43.2

$\chi^2 = 4.84$ 1 df $p < 0.05$

As in the case of the decisions of the consultative panels, it is important to analyse the outcome in relation to the nature of offences committed. For the purposes of this analysis the first court dispositions are taken into account. Accepting that a simple comparison of gender with court disposal indicates no statistically significant difference (Table 5.1b), this assumption would only be valid if the nature of offences charged were similar for males and females. A number of variables are, therefore, examined in the following section in order to arrive at some assessment of the comparability of the offences charged in the male and female sub-samples. Similar variables to those used in the section on the consultative panels are examined, namely: the type of offence charged; the monetary value ascribed to the offence; the numbers of offences charged; the frequency of offending; the age of the young offender; the previous offending pattern; and whether the offences were committed jointly or alone.

Type of offence charged

Table 5.3 shows the distribution of offences charged between the male and female sub-samples. Since a number of young people committed more than one offence, the total number of offences charged is greater than the number of cases in the sample. Because of the small numbers in some of the categories, the chi-square calculation was based only on those categories where the numbers were larger, excluding category 13, as this was a composite category of different offences and therefore not directly comparable between the gender sub-samples. The categories included in the calculation were 3, 5, 6, 8 and 12. For a comparison of these categories (χ^2 = 45.89; 4 df; p < 0.00) the chi-square figure was significant.

Table 5.3   Sex, by type of offence charged

						Category of offence								Row total
		1	2	3	4	5	6	7	8	9	10	11	12	13	
Male	no.	10	1	31	2	25	10	2	16	2	4	2	21	13	147
	%	6.8	0.7	21.1	1.4	17.0	6.8	1.4	10.9	1.4	2.7	1.4	14.2	14.2	100
Female	no.	4	4	15	0	20	40	4	13	0	0	3	5	13	121
	%	3.3	3.3	12.4	0	16.5	33.1	3.3	10.8	0	0	2.5	4.1	10.7	100

Key:
1, violence against the person; 2, sexual offences; 3, burglary; 4, robbery; 5, theft and handling; 6, theft from store; 7, fraud and forgery; 8, criminal damage; 9, arson; 10, threatening behaviour; 11, offences involving alcohol; 12, theft of motor vehicle; 13, other.

This significant difference in the type of offences committed by males and females differs from the evidence of self-report studies discussed in Chapter 2, but not from national statistics for England and Wales (Figure 5.1). The reasons for this difference between self-report and official statistics have been discussed already and possibly point to gender bias operating at reporting and arrest stages in the identification of a delinquent young person.

Although there appears to be a significant difference in the type of offences charged between the male and female sub-samples, the fact that the difference in the court dispositions between these two groups was not significant might suggest that some gender bias was operating. The nature of this bias might be explored through an examination of the remaining variables, mostly concerned with assessing the seriousness of offending patterns, but also with the ages of the young people involved.

Cross-tabulations of gender by court disposition controlling for type of offence were carried out. Where figures permitted (some of the

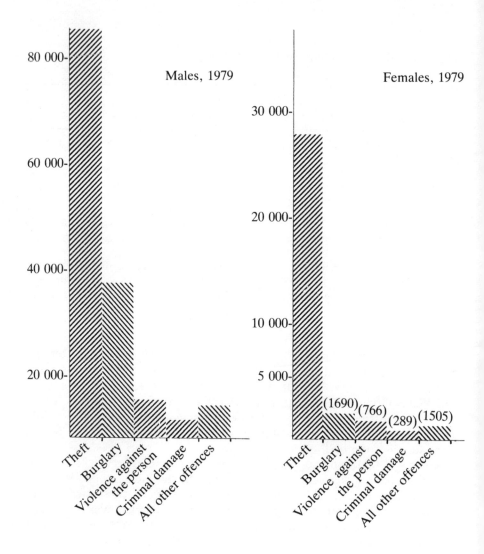

Source: DHSS, 1981, p.21, table 9.

Figure 5.1 Types of offences for which juveniles are cautioned or sentenced

figures in some categories were too small), chi-square values were calculated, but no statistically significant probability levels were obtained.

Value ascribed to offence charged

One way of measuring the seriousness of an offence is by the monetary value involved in property offences, whether of goods stolen or handled or of property damaged. Where the monetary value of the offence was known, cases were allocated to one of four groups and these grouped values of offences charged were cross-tabulated by gender (Table 5.4). In 59 cases it was not applicable to ascribe a value to the offence and these cases have been omitted. As can be seen from the table, the distribution of the figures is fairly even and the chi-square figure indicates that there is no statistically significant difference between the male and female samples. Further cross-tabulations of gender by court disposition controlling for value of offence charged were carried out, and where figures permitted, chi-square values were calculated. No statistically significant results were obtained.

Table 5.4 Sex, by value of offence charged

		Not known	£1–£5	£6–£25	£26–£100	Over £100	Row total
Male	no.	14	6	17	12	14	63
	%	22.2	9.5	27.0	19.0	22.2	45.0
Female	no.	21	5	21	18	12	77
	%	27.3	6.5	27.3	24.3	15.6	55.0

$\chi^2 = 1.88$ 4 df   p = n.s.

Thus it appears from these data that the seriousness of property offences as measured by the monetary value ascribed to the offences was not statistically significant in the difference between male and female sub-samples.

Number of offences charged

Another indication of the seriousness of the offending pattern of the young person might be gained from an examination of the number of offences with which the young person was charged at the court appearance. This, in turn, might affect the disposals for the male and female groups if it appears that one or other group has a more serious offending pattern.

Cross-tabulations of gender by number of offences charged show no significant difference between the male and female sub-samples (Table 5.5), and the conclusion to be drawn is that using these criteria it is not possible to say that one or other group commits more serious offences than the other.

Table 5.5   Sex, by number of offences charged

| | No. of offences charged | | | |
	1	2–4	5+	Row total
Male	52	35	13	100
Female	52	41	6	99

$\chi^2 = 3.11$ 2 df   p = n.s.

Joint offending

This variable is introduced for two reasons. First, in attempting to assess the comparative seriousness of offending of the male and female groups in the sample, it might be assumed that magistrates would see as more serious group or gang delinquency than offences which were committed singly or in pairs. The second reason for its introduction is with reference to the discussion on the nature of female delinquency outlined in Chapter 1. There it was seen that female delinquency is often considered to be 'disturbed' rather than deviant behaviour, whereas male delinquency is more inclined to be seen in terms of cultural deviancy. Table 5.6 shows the distribution of offences committed either alone or with numbers up to eight others. It can be observed that three females and no males are found in the two highest categories. Fewer females commit offences alone, more often offending with one other person. In order to calculate the chi-square figure for this table, it was collapsed into three columns: offences committed alone, with one other person or with two or more people. There was found to be no statistically significant difference between the gender groups ($\chi^2 = 4.51$; 2 df; p = n.s.). These results would lend little support for the stereotype views of male and female delinquency; girls appear to commit offences in the company of others as much as boys. The data lend no support either to the view that one group has more serious offending patterns.

Table 5.6   Sex, by number of friends involved in offence charged

| | | \multicolumn{9}{c}{No. of friends} |
		0	1	2	3	4	5	6	8	Row total
Male	no.	31	40	17	7	2	3	0	0	100
	%	31.0	40.0	17.0	7.0	2.0	3.0	0	0	51.0
Female	no.	22	53	14	4	0	0	1	2	96
	%	22.9	55.2	14.6	4.2	0	0	1.0	2.1	49.0

Previous offending pattern

Previous offending is often taken into consideration by magistrates, thus under this heading the number, nature and frequency of previous offences are compared for the male and female sub-samples. Table 5.7 shows the distribution of numbers of previous offences. It can be seen that more females (26.7 per cent) than males (19.8 per cent) were first offenders and that more females appear in the one previous offence category. Males are more heavily represented in the last two columns, representing two to five previous offences and more than six. Frequency counts showed that one male had seventeen previous offences, and one female had sixteen previous offences. However, although represented across the range from 0–16 previous offences, the larger

Table 5.7   Sex, by number of previous offences

	0	1	2–5	6+	Row total
Male	37	18	21	22	98
Female	50	22	9	6	88

$\chi^2 = 15.89$ 3df   p $<$0.01

number of females are clearly weighted to the lower end of the range and this is reflected in the significance of the chi-square figure. Overall it appears that the female sub-sample consisted of less serious offenders on the criterion of number of previous offences.

First offenders and court disposal

In order to assess whether first-offender status influenced court disposal, cross-tabulations of gender by court disposal controlling for numbers of offences were obtained. It might be assumed that if gender bias were operating, it would be seen most clearly in the first-offender groups. However, gender by court disposal controlling for the previous offences (Table 5.8) showed no statistically significant difference. The calculations were limited to the three main disposals in order to main-tain higher numbers in the cells for the purpose of the chi-square calculation, and also because detention and attendance centre disposals are not directly comparable for the female sample.

Table 5.8   Sex, by court disposal: first offenders

	Conditional discharge	Fine	Supervision Order	Row total
Male	14	11	9	34
Female	26	6	13	45
Total				79

χ^2 = 4.03   2 df   p = n.s.

These findings suggest some inequality of treatment. Whilst there are more female first offenders in the sample and there appears to be no overall significant difference in the treatment of males and females (Table 5.1b), it would suggest harsher treatment of the female group.

The nature of previous offences showed a different pattern from the type of current offence charged (see Table 5.3). Table 5.9 shows the distribution of offences committed prior to the offences for which they are currently appearing in court. Shoplifting features less significantly for the female sample than in the distribution for current offences, and over the three categories (3, 5 and 8) where larger numbers permitted a chi-square calculation, there was no significant difference between the male and female sample (χ^2 = 1.98; 2 df; p = n.s.).

Table 5.9 Sex, by type of previous offences

		\multicolumn{13}{c}{Category of offence}												Row total
		1	2	3	4	5	6	7	8	9	10	11	12	13	
Male	no.	6	0	30	1	34	1	4	13	0	1	1	9	13	113
	%	5.3	0	26.5	0.9	30.1	0.9	3.5	11.5	0	0.9	0.9	8.0	11.5	100.0
Female	no.	0	2	8	0	18	2	3	6	0	1	1	1	3	45
	%	0	4.4	17.9	0	40.0	4.4	6.7	13.3	0	2.2	2.2	2.2	6.7	100.0

$\chi^2 = 1.98$ 2 df   p = n.s.

Key:
1, violence against the person; 2, sexual offences; 3, burglary; 4, robbery; 5, theft and handling; 6, theft from store; 7, fraud and forgery; 8, criminal damage; 9, arson; 10, threatening behaviour; 11, offences involving consumption of alcohol; 12, theft of motor vehicle; 13, other.

With regard to frequency in the pattern of previous offending, male and female cases were compared on the basis of time between their first court appearance and the present court appearance (Table 5.10). No significant difference was observed between the two groups.

With regard to the pattern of previous offending, therefore, a mixed picture emerges of a female sub-sample consisting of a significantly larger number of first offenders, and with fewer cases represented in the range of number of offences, yet on the other hand, with no significant difference in the type of offence committed or of the time-span of offending.

Table 5.10 Sex, by time between first and present court appearances

	Under 12 months	Over 12 months	Row total
Male	18	33	95
Female	11	15	83

$\chi^2 = 0.37$ 1 df   p = n.s.

In the previous section it was shown that national statistics indicate that age is an important factor in the decision as to whether to caution a young offender or whether to proceed with charges. Figures for England and Wales show (DHSS, 1981, p.19) that the peak age for offending for females has been 14 since 1962, but for males it shifted in 1972 from 14 to 15. The school leaving age was raised from 15 to 16 in this year and possibly contributes to this change.

In the present sample Table 5.11 shows the distribution of ages for the total sample and for the gender sub-samples. It can be observed that the minimum age for males in the sample is a year younger than that for females. In order to test the significance of any difference in the distribution of ages, the sample was divided into a younger group, consisting of all cases with ages up to 13 years 11 months, and an older group of all cases from 14 years upwards. Table 5.12 shows that although most of the sample fell into the older age-group, there was no significant difference shown when these age-groups were cross-tabulated with gender. Further cross-tabulations of sex by court disposition controlling for age-group were carried out and in both age-groups there was no statistically significant association (younger, $\chi^2 = 0.24$ 1 df $p = $ n.s.; older, $\chi^2 = 4.78$ 5 df $p = $ n.s.).

Table 5.11   Age range

	All	Males	Females
Mean age	15.3	15.4	15.2
Minimum age	10.11	10.9	11.9
Maximum age	17.2	17.1	17.1

The conclusion to be drawn from this data is that there was no significant difference in the age of the gender sub-samples; and also that age appears to have little direct influence on court disposition for either sex.

Summary: court disposals

In this section the relationship between gender and court disposals has been explored and also the possible influence of a number of variables which might influence the court's decisions. These are summarized in

Table 5.12   Grouped age, by sex

		Younger (10–13)	Older (14–17)	Row total
Male	no.	16	84	100
	%	8.0	42.2	50.3
Female	no.	21	78	99
	%	10.6	39.2	49.7

$\chi^2 = 0.58$ 1 df   p = n.s.

Table 5.13. The data show that whilst the number of females who received conditional discharges was greater than the number of males, this difference was not statistically significant. However, this apparent similarity in the disposals for males and females does not necessarily mean that these groups were receiving similar treatment since factors such as the type and seriousness of the offence charged, the previous record and the age of the young person would be factors taken into account by the court. Gender comparisons for a number of factors aiming to assess the seriousness of the offence (the monetary value ascribed to the offence, the number of offences charged and joint offending) were all found to show no significant difference between the gender sub-samples. With regard to the previous record, the nature of previous offences and the timespan between court appearances also showed no significant difference between the gender groups. Age also produced no significant differences between the male and female groups. The two factors which were found to differ significantly between the two groups were, first, certain categories of offences (burglary, theft and handling, shoplifting, criminal damage and theft of motor vehicle), and secondly, the number of first offenders; there were significantly more first offenders in the female group than in the male group. There appeared to be no significant difference in the treatment of first offenders, but overall it might be suggested that a definite feature emerging from the data is the significantly greater number of female first offenders in the sample. Similar treatment of males and females as suggested by the figure in Table 5.1b would, therefore, imply a harsher treatment of females in the overall group. Care must be taken, however, to ensure that only such conclusions are drawn as are justified by the data, and the fact that other variables showed no significant difference between the gender sub-samples needs to be balanced against the likelihood of gender bias operating against the interests of females before the courts. However, there is sufficient evidence to question a too ready assumption on the part of those who work in relation to the juvenile courts that the courts are more favourably disposed towards females.

Table 5.13 Summary of findings: gender and court dispositions

Comparison	Outcome
1 Gender by main disposal	Not significant
2 Gender by second disposal	Significant in favour of females
3 Gender by type of offence	Significant difference in certain categories
4 Gender by seriousness of offence:	
value of offence	Not significant
number of offences charged	Not significant
joint offending	Not significant
5 Gender by previous offences:	
number of previous offences	Significant
nature of previous offences	Not significant
pattern of previous offences	Not significant
6 Gender by age of young offender	Not significant

II Gender and family structure and socio-economic status

The research evidence relating to delinquency and broken homes has been reviewed in Chapter 2, and highlighted the fact that much of the research was carried out on already institutionalized samples, thus building bias into the figures. Not surprisingly, therefore, many of the studies show high percentages for cases with broken homes. The evidence has also suggested that more delinquent girls come from broken homes than boys, although it was pointed out that a number of studies dispute this. This evidence has also fed into the view of female delinquency as stemming from psychiatric disturbance resulting from poor family experience, whilst male delinquency in the popular view is more often seen to result from 'getting into bad company', that is, is culturally based. The emphasis on welfare and medical models in the response to female delinquency and its implications has also been discussed. The present study explored a number of variables related to the family background and socio-economic status of the young people appearing before the court.

Family background

For each case the young person's permanent home at the time of the court appearance was established: 47 per cent of the male sample and 50 per cent of the female sample came from broken homes in the sense that they were not living with their natural parents living together. Table 5.14 shows the remarkably even distribution between the gender sub-samples for this variable and indicates quite clearly no significant gender difference in the rate of broken homes. It can also be seen that 27 per cent of the male sample and 21.4 per cent of the female sample came from single-parent families.

Table 5.14 Sex, by permanent home

	Natural parents living together	Mother living alone	Father living alone	Natural parent remarried or cohabiting	Other relative	Other	Row total
Male	53	16	11	14	2	4	100
Female	49	18	3	16	3	9	98

It was recognized that although the young person's permanent home may have been considered to be with their natural parents living together at the time of the court appearance, this would not necessarily exclude the possibility of the young person having been in substitute care at some time. The distribution of cases across the various forms of substitute care are seen in Table 5.15a, and again remarkable similarity between the gender sub-samples is evident, supporting closely the evidence relating to permanent home.

The categories are very similar for males and females, but it can be seen from the table that institutionalized females were more often placed in a children's home, whilst males were more often placed in a community home school with education (CHE) on the premises. The recent closure of many CHEs would change that trend for young people currently appearing before the courts.

In order to test the significance of any gender differences observable

Table 5.15a   Sex, by substitute care

	No substitute care	Assessment Centre	Children's Home	Foster care	CHE	With relative	Other	Row total
Male	40	23	8	2	15	7	5	100
Female	47	20	16	2	5	4	5	98

Table 5.15b   Sex, by substitute care (grouped)

	No substitute care	Institutional substitute care	Other substitute care	Row total
Male	40	46	14	100
Female	47	41	11	99

$\chi^2 = 1.19$ 2 df   p = n.s.

in the table, the columns were collapsed (Table 5.15b) into three: no substitute care experienced by the young person; institutional care of some kind (i.e. assessment centre, children's home or CHE); and other substitute care including foster care and care with a relative. No statistically significant difference between the gender groups was evident from the data.

Family size and parental age was another variable examined in the present study. Previous research studies have produced conflicting evidence, and this has been reviewed in Chapter 2; the existence of very few gender comparative studies in this area emerged from the review. Family size was compared for the male and female group in relation, first, to the number of siblings (Table 5.16), and secondly, to the number of children living in the home at the time of the court appearance (Table 5.17). The reason for the numbers in some of the columns in Table 5.17 being greater than those in Table 5.16 would be the existence of step-siblings and possibly some foster children living with the families in the sample. For some cases the information was not available and hence the row totals do not correspond with total numbers in the sample. An interesting feature from this latter table is the very few young people of either sex who are only children. Table 5.17 shows similarity between the gender groups for the numbers of children living in the family home. It can be seen that over 60 per cent of young people in each gender group come from moderately sized families of two, three and four children.

Table 5.16   Sex, by number of siblings

	0	1	2	3	4	5+	Row total
Male	3	17	26	22	20	12	88
Female	6	15	17	23	21	16	98

Table 5.17   Sex, by number of children living in family home

	Including subject	2	3	4	5	6+	Row total
Male	8	22	24	20	16	10	100
Female	8	22	18	21	21	7	97

Another variable examined in relation to family background was the existence of delinquent and criminal activity within the family. In order to assess this, parental criminal record was noted. Here, however, reliance on the knowledge of the probation officer or social worker currently working with the family means that the reliability of these data may be open to question: spent or other criminal records may well have existed in families unknown to the social workers or probation officers. The numbers involved are too small to draw definite conclusions, but there is little evidence of any large gender difference (Table 5.18).

The numbers of siblings at risk for various reasons, or who may have had a delinquent record, were identified by reporting the number of siblings who were known to either the probation service or the social services department. No significant gender difference was indicated (Table 5.19). It can be seen that around half of each gender sample came from families where none of their siblings were known to the department. Very few of the young people in the sample — only four boys and seven girls — were jointly charged with siblings at their court appearance.

One factor which might lead to complicated family dynamics and

Table 5.18 Sex, by parental criminal record

		Prison	Other sentence	Both	Row total
Male	mother	1	5	0	
	father	1	3	4	14
Female	mother	0	4	0	
	father	7	2	6	19

Table 5.19 Number of siblings known to probation and social services

	0	1	2+	Row total
Male	53	21	7	81
Female	45	15	14	74

$\chi^2 = 2.09$ 2 df   p = n.s.

the problem of appropriate role models for the young people might be the existence of either very old or very young parents in the group. Table 5.20, showing the distribution of parental ages, might suggest a trend for mothers to be on average younger than fathers for each gender group, but this would be expected, and there is again remarkable similarity between the male and female groups. Bearing in mind that the mean age of the sample (see Table 5.11) was 15.4 for males and 15.2 for females, there appears to be little evidence from Table 5.20 to suggest a large number of particularly young or old parents in either group.

Involvement of welfare agencies

Thus far the evidence has suggested no significant difference between the gender groups for a number of variables associated with family background. In the light of this evidence the allocation of young people to either social services or probation shows an interesting gender bias. Table 5.21 refers to the agency completing the Social Inquiry Report for the court, or by whom the case records are held, or to whom a supervision order is given. The data lend support to the view which

Table 5.20   Parental ages

		Under 30	31–40	41–50	51–60	61 and over
Male	mother	2	34	30	8	0
	father	0	14	42	15	1
Female	mother	2	31	27	8	1
	father	0	16	24	15	2

suggests that a welfare interpretation of delinquency operates in respect of females, and a justice interpretation in respect of males, in so far as social services might be seen as a welfare-oriented agency and the probation service with its closer link with the courts as a justice-oriented agency.

Table 5.21   Sex, by agency

	Probation	SSD	Row total
Male	62	38	100
Female	45	53	98

$\chi^2 = 4.53$ 1 df $p < 0.05$

It can be seen that the clear trend is for more female cases to be dealt with by social services and for more male cases to be dealt with by probation. The chi-square figure indicates a statistically significant difference. Had there been significant differences in either the age-group or the family backgrounds of males and females, then this difference may have been expected. It has been shown that these differences are not evident from the data of the present study, and it must be assumed that the allocation of cases is influenced by the views of female delinquency outlined in Chapter 1, that is, as 'disturbance' and warranting a welfare-oriented approach. Undoubtedly, the present data shows evidence of families where a welfare approach would be appropriate because of the number of broken families or siblings offending or at risk, but the important point is that this was no different for boys. The evidence from Table 5.21 seems to be either that boys are discriminated against in this respect or that girls are labelled 'disturbed' to their disadvantage.

Socio-economic status

In this section comparisons are made between the gender sub-samples of the young person's employment pattern, parental employment, parental income and housing. Table 5.22 shows the numbers in employment or at school at the time of their court appearance. Information was not available for one female.

Table 5.22   Young person's employment status

	At school	Employed	Unemployed	Row total
Male	66	19	15	100
Female	73	7	18	98

$\chi^2 = 6.14$ 2 df $p < 0.05$

There is a significant difference observable between the male and female groups, though this is due more to the larger numbers of females still at school rather than any gender difference in the unemployed column. The proportion of unemployed young people may be lower than expected because the data were collected before the recent steep rise in unemployment rates for both adults and school-leavers in England and Wales. Of those young people who were employed, four males and three females had had one previous job and one male and three females had had two previous jobs. Of those young people who were unemployed, thirteen had been unemployed for under six months and two for over six months. For females the figures were eight unemployed for under six months and nine for over six months. A number of young people who were unemployed at the time of their court appearance had had no job since leaving school, including twelve males and sixteen females. These reflect a high proportion of those unemployed.

No definite conclusion can be drawn from these data because of the small numbers involved. The larger number of girls who remained at school may be due to the age factor, although with the mean age of the sample showing a difference of only 2 months (see Table 5.11) this is unlikely, or it may be due to a trend for girls to stay on at school because of lack of employment prospects.

Working mothers were clearly not a factor in any gender differences in the sample. Table 5.23 shows a very similar distribution for both groups.

Table 5.23   Sex, by mother's employment

	Full time	Part time	Unemployed	Not employed outside the home	Row total
Male	20	12	15	41	88
Female	17	14	11	42	84

$\chi^2 = 0.93$ 3 df   p = n.s.

Unemployed fathers featured significantly in the sample as a whole. They consisted of 50.9 per cent of cases (159 cases) where the father's employment was known, whereas the unemployment rates for the research locations were 11.6 per cent in the city and 12.1 per cent in the town. The national average at the time was 9.8 per cent. This 50.9 per cent figure is therefore very high, but significantly the unemployed fathers were distributed almost equally between the gender sub-samples (Table 5.24).

Table 5.24   Sex, by father's employment

	Full time	Unemployed	Retired	Row total
Male	40	40	2	82
Female	32	41	0	73

A crude analysis of the status of fathers' employment was undertaken. The Registrar-General's classification of occupations was used as a guide and a simplified list of five categories produced: professional; intermediate occupations; skilled occupations, including technical skills; partly skilled; and unskilled. Table 5.25 shows a similarity in the distribution between the gender groups, with a concentration in each case on the skilled and partly skilled categories. This would place most of the young people, predictably, in the working-class and lower-middle-class groups. As indicated by the row totals, only about one-third of each sub-sample are represented, the unemployed category having been excluded, and data being unavailable for 19 male and 37 female cases.

Table 5.25   Sex, by status of father's occupation

	Professional	Intermediate	Skilled	Partly skilled	Unskilled	Row total
Male	2	4	21	10	2	39
Female	2	1	16	9	2	30

Families in receipt of supplementary benefit were identified. Twenty-four families in the male sample and 34 families in the female sample were in receipt. Allowing for 15 missing observations, this left 69 families in the male sample and 57 families in the female sample not in receipt. The chi-square figure for these differences was not significant ($\chi^2 = 2.34$; 1 df; p = n.s.).

House ownership was recorded as an indicator of socio-economic status. Here significantly less of the female sample came from owner-occupied households (30 male and 19 female households were owner-occupied). There was less difference between gender groups for the rented housing families (63 male and 71 female households lived in rented housing). Overall, however, the difference between the gender sub-samples was significant ($\chi^2 = 5.74$; 1 df; p < 0.05). The larger number in the rented households category were for rented council housing, only six households in the male sub-sample and one household in the female sub-sample renting privately; that is, 54 per cent of the male sample and 65 per cent of the female sample lived in rented council housing.

House ownership was the variable which showed the clearest difference between the gender sub-samples in this section. Other factors relating to the young person's employment and to parental employment status and income were found to be not significantly different.

Summary of findings

The overall impression from a comparison of the male and female sub-samples in the present study is of similarity rather than differences between the two groups. With regard to family background, the incidence of broken homes, family size as measured by number of siblings and by the number of children currently living in the home, parental criminal record and siblings known to probation and social services departments, the ages of parents were all found to show no significant differences in a comparison of male and female sub-samples. The incidence of substitute care was not different overall, though there was a trend for institutionalized girls to be in children's homes and institutionalized boys to be in community homes with education (CHEs). Despite the lack of difference in family background, significantly more girls were referred to social services and more boys for probation.

Similar results were obtained from comparison of the gender sub-samples for variables associated with socio-economic status. Although more girls were found to be still at school, similar numbers of girls and boys in the group were unemployed. No significant difference was found between the groups for parental unemployment, or for the status of fathers' job. There was, however, a much higher rate of unemployment overall in the sample than either the local rate of unemployment at that time in each location or the national rate. There was no significant gender difference in families identified as receiving supplementary benefit. House occupation was the only significant factor; more females came from families who rented council accommodation, and more males came from families who were owner-occupiers.

III. Gender and location

It was suggested in Chapter 4 that the data from the consultative panels implied the interpretation that female delinquency in the town location of the research might be regarded as more serious than in the city, using recidivism as an indicator of seriousness. This section compares female offending in the town and the city, using a number of variables as indicators of seriousness.

Age was the first variable explored. There is evidence from research studies that the younger the age at which children first appear before the courts, the more serious their delinquent career is likely to be. On a comparison of older (14–17) and younger (10–13) female age-groups for the city and town locations no significance was found ($\chi^2 = 0.30$; 1 df; p = n.s.).

The number of offences charged was compared for the town and city group as another indicator of seriousness of offending. A few cases were found in the categories of 6+ offences, but they were too few to influence the comparison, and the chi-square calculation was based on the larger numbers in the groups shown in Table 5.26.

Previous offending can be a useful indicator of seriousness of offending and numbers of previous offences were compared for females in each location (Table 5.27). It can be seen that each location had the same number of first offenders, and although the city location had five offenders in the higher categories, whilst the town had none, the numbers were too small from which to draw conclusions other than to note the trend.

Table 5.26 Location, by number of offences charged (females)

	Number of offences charged		
	1	2–5	Row total
City	23	23	46
Town	29	20	49

$\chi^2 = 0.87$ 1 df   p = n.s.

Table 5.27 Location, by number of previous offences (females)

	Number of previous offences									
	0	1	2	3	6	7	8	9	16	Row total
City	25	10	0	3	1	2	1	1	1	44
Town	25	13	5	1	0	0	0	0	0	44

Joint offending was also examined in each location. Ten city females and seven town females were charged alone, and 39 city females and 40 town females were jointly charged with others for the offences for which they appeared. Clearly, no significant difference is evident.

On the evidence of these variables, therefore, it appears that there is no evidence to suggest that female offending is more serious in the town than in the city.

6 Summary and conclusions

The research reported in the preceding chapters examined two stages in the decision-making process in the juvenile justice system: the police consultative panels and the juvenile court in two locations, a city and a small town. Male and female samples were compared for evidence of gender bias in the decision-making process at each level: for location differences and for differences in social background. Detailed summaries of these findings are included in the appropriate section in earlier chapters. The intention in this section is to review the overall results and address their possible implications.

The present study: main findings

The consultative panels

One clear feature emerging from the data on the consultative panels is that more girls than boys overall receive cautions. However, on further examination of the data it appears that this conclusion does not hold true when the data for the town location are analysed separately: the significance in the gender difference disappears. A number of variables were introduced to assess their relationship with gender and with the panels' recommendations. It was found that females were treated more harshly than males for offences against the person, but that younger girls were treated more leniently than younger boys. Previous record was more important than gender in influencing panel recommendations, so that both males and females with a previous record were recommended for court proceedings rather than a caution. Regarding gender bias and the agencies involved, there seemed to be some evidence of this operating before the panel stage, with a larger number of the girls in the sample appearing to be known to the police but not brought before the panels. Education Welfare Officers tended to comment more positively on girls than on boys.

Findings from the data on the consultative panels not related to gender differences were interesting to note. There appeared to be little sense in which the welfare agencies (probation, social services and education welfare) acted as advocates for the young people or for a 'softer' approach to juvenile justice. This evidence differs from the popular public image, particularly of social workers. Nor was the image of a 'hard' police approach to juvenile crime borne out in the comments made by the police in the panels, although overall the panels may be said to have taken a fairly 'hard' approach in recommending either cautions or proceedings for every offender. This is despite the fact that many of the juveniles in the sample fell into the younger age-group (10—13) and were first-time petty offenders. Diversion from the juvenile justice system appeared not to have a part in policy influencing the functioning of the panels.

Thus the findings from the data on the consultative panels are interesting in relation to diversion policies, to the role of the welfare agencies and also the nature of gender bias. It was seen that gender bias was not a simple and straightforward function of the 'chivalry' approach to young offenders, but that it is a more complex phenomenon than is generally assumed. This apparent complexity in the nature of gender bias operating in the juvenile justice system in the research locations was also reflected by the data collected from the juvenile court section.

The juvenile courts

Findings from the juvenile court data showed, unexpectedly, no significant difference in a comparison of the main dispositions with gender. Further analysis of other variables relating to type of offence, seriousness of offence, history of previous offending and age showed significant gender difference only in certain types of offence, and in the number of previous offences committed. Other measures of the seriousness of offences, such as value ascribed to the offence charged, the number of offences charged and joint offending, showed no significant gender differences. However, there was evidence of gender bias in the second dispositions given by the court in some cases — these usually being where more than one offence was charged — in that females appeared to receive more lenient treatment. Overall the fact that there were significantly more first offenders in the female sample set alongside the lack of significant gender difference in the main court dispositions would suggest that females were not equally treated, but were treated more harshly than the males in the study.

Findings on family background of the young offenders in the sample showed no significant gender difference in broken homes, family size, parental or sibling criminal activity, or the ages of parents. No significant gender difference was observed overall in the incidence of some kind of substitute care, although there were observable differences within the institutional care category, showing that females were more often placed in children's homes and males more often placed in community homes with education on the premises. This might suggest a more lenient approach to females. Despite the lack of difference in family background, significantly more girls were referred to social services and more boys to the probation service, suggesting a trend towards a welfare approach to delinquency in girls and a justice approach to delinquency in boys.

An examination of the data relating to socio-economic status showed overall no significant gender difference on a number of variables, with the exception that more females came from families renting council property. Unemployment showed no significant difference between the gender sub-samples on either the young people's employment status or that of their parents. Significantly, however, unemployment within the sample generally was considerably higher than both the local and national figures relating to the time at which the research took place.

There was no evidence to suggest that with regard to location differences female offending was any more serious in the city location than in the town location. Indeed, from the evidence of cases considered by the consultative panels, it appeared that there was a small group of female recidivists in the town; and if recidivism is used as a factor on which an estimation of the seriousness of offending is partly based, then it might be said that female offending was more serious in the small town location than in the city location.

The research hypotheses

In the light of this evidence from the data it will be apparent that the research hypotheses are not upheld. This is an important overall finding from the research since the hypotheses were formulated to represent the most widely accepted views of many of those who work in relation to the juvenile courts and the police cautioning system. The fact that none of them are fully supported by the data indicates that the assumptions about female delinquency upon which many welfare and other workers operate need challenging and revising.

Social background of the young offender
and attitudes to female delinquency

The hypothesis receiving clearest rejection from the study is the view that there would be significant differences in the social and economic backgrounds between the gender sub-samples. This was clearly not so, the overall impression being one of similarity rather than differences. This has important implications for the way in which female delinquency is viewed, discussed in the following section. The lack of significant gender difference in the socio-economic status of the young people in the sample confirms the findings of May (1977), whose data also showed in this respect more similarities than differences between males and females. With regard to 'broken homes', May found that in his Aberdeen study girls whose fathers had died were more than twice as likely to appear in court than the average Aberdeen girl, though this difference was not apparent for boys. May acknowledges that the numbers are very small (N = 5), but nevertheless claims it offers 'some support for the generally held belief that the impact of the broken home is felt more keenly by girls than by boys' (ibid., p.207). However, this is too crude a measure of the idea of the 'broken home' when we live in a society where separation, divorce and cohabitation are increasingly common, and where a young person may experience living in a family group with step-parents and siblings, single parents and cohabitation. The present research aimed to allow for this variety, and yet found no statistical difference in the permanent home situation of males and females (see Table 5.14) or in the amount of substitute care received (see Table 5.15a).

These results reflect the findings of Weeks's (1940) study, which suggested that the association of broken homes with female delinquency was associated with type of offence, in particular, status offences such as incorrigibility, being in moral danger and running away from home. Later studies, such as Grygier *et al.* (1969), Riege (1972) and Datesman, Scarpitti and Stephenson (1975), all support Weeks's findings. However, there does remain a number of studies discussed earlier (Wattenberg and Saunders, 1954; Gibbons and Griswold, 1957; Morris, 1964; O'Kelly, 1965; Andrew, 1976; Caplan *et al.*, 1980) which found an association between female delinquents and broken homes. Clearly, more research, using larger samples and matched control groups with the normal population, is required but the clear message of the findings of the present study examining both permanent home and substitute care as a variable cannot be ignored.

The broken home with its supposed consequent psychological problems, affecting girls in particular, has fuelled the theoretical view of female criminality and delinquency which emphasizes the disturbed mental state of female offenders: Cowie, Cowie and Slater (1968); Pollok and Friedman (1969); Konopka (1966); Vedder and Somerville (1970); Trèse (1962); and the classic study of Thomas (1923), have all emphasized this approach to understanding female delinquency, following in the well-established tradition of Lombroso and Ferraro (1895), the Gluecks (1934) and Pollok (1961), and their influence has been discussed earlier. Findings from studies such as the present one, and from recent contributions to the literature, such as that of Chesney-Lind (1973), Campbell (1981), Smart (1976), Steffensmeir (1980) and others discussed in Chapter 1, all challenge this idea of female crime which has been for too long accepted by those who work with female offenders.

Other findings in the comparison of social backgrounds of the male and female young offenders in the present study showed that there was no evidence that females came from larger families or had particularly young parents. These are factors which might be associated by some with family instability.

The nature and pattern of female delinquency

The hypothesis that male and female juveniles will differ significantly with regard to the nature and pattern of offending was not completely refuted by the evidence from the present study, but the data serve to warn against too easy an acceptance of such long-held views. May (1977) found in his comparison of male and female offending that 70 per cent of the female sample consisted of theft, though his research design did not indicate what proportion of this was shoplifting, and he found a significant difference in the pattern of male and female offending. Certainly, the present research found statistically significant differences in some of the categories with female shoplifters in the city sample being very apparent. Yet on a closer comparison of the value of property offences, the number of offences charged and joint offending there was no significant gender difference. One of the problems in comparing offences by type, based as were the categories in the present study on the categories used by the Home Office for the *Criminal Statistics*, is that gender bias is already built in to many offence categories such as taking and driving away a motor vehicle without permission of the owner. Gender-role expectations and sexist education ensures that an adolescent male is more likely to possess the skills of starting a motor vehicle without an ignition key, and having started it, of driving it away, than his female counterpart. Gender bias operating well before the juvenile enters the justice system may mean that store detectives are more likely to expect females to shoplift than males and that their attitudes may well be reflected in the greater number of females arrested for this offence.

The present study, whilst showing evidence of difference in type of offence as categorized, nevertheless lends some support to the self-report studies reviewed in Chapter 2, which indicate that whilst there are differences in male and female delinquency patterns, those differences are not as large as official criminal statistics suggest.

Location differences between town and city

The hypothesis that female offending could be more serious in the city than in the town was clearly refuted by the evidence in the present study. Indeed there was some evidence to suggest that female offending was more serious in the town. This conclusion based on the finding that there were more female recidivists in the town needs to be regarded with caution, however, since it may be a function of youngsters already identified as offenders in a small town being more apparent, and thus more open to further arrests and charges, than they would be in the relative anonymity of the city.

Gender bias in decision-making in the judicial process

The hypothesis that females would always be treated more leniently than males was not supported by the data. The findings from this study show that gender bias does exist in the operation of the juvenile justice system, but that it is a rather complex affair, sometimes operating in favour of females and sometimes against. May (1977) drew a tentative conclusion from the data available from his study that the courts showed a 'slight tendency' to deal more severely with females; the present study analyses gender bias in more detail and at two levels in the system. Webb (1984) also found evidence of gender bias in the British courts. The finding in the present study, that females charged with offences in the category of violence against the person are dealt with more severely, suggests that the female is harshly punished in our society for violation of traditional gender-role expectations. Thus the evidence from the present study is in line with the findings of the numerous American studies which are summarized along with the one or two British studies in Table 2.8. This table shows studies undertaken at different stages of the judicial process, and the clear picture which emerges from the discussion in Chapter 2 is that there is an overall picture of clear gender bias at work.

The data indicating gender bias in the present study are less clear than some of the studies indicated in Table 2.8, e.g. Chesney-Lind (1973), because of the deliberate omission of cases appearing on care proceedings. The present study was limited to criminal proceedings where issues about the sexualization of female offending are not as apparent.

Implications of the findings

Juvenile justice and social policy

The findings from this gender comparative study of the processing of male and female juvenile offenders in Britain support those who have an increasing concern about the incompatibility of welfare and justice in the juvenile court system (e.g. Thorpe et al., 1980; Morris and Giller, 1983; Morris et al., 1980; Osborne, 1984). The implementation of the Children and Young Persons Act 1969, it is now widely recognized, has had the unintended consequence of producing a more punitive juvenile system. More young people than ever are sentenced to periods of custodial detention. This is all despite the welfare orientation and intention of the Act: 'Rampant discretion, in an area so politically important as the social control of working class youth has over the past decade led to a major dissonance between the intentions of the uncut Act and the actual sentencing patterns produced' (Parker et al., 1981, p.242).

The dichotomy of welfare and justice is worked out practically in individual cases over issues of care and control or punishment and treatment. The great danger of the welfare model is its use of 'treatment', and the medical model at the expense of the rights of the young person. In the welfare system young people may be deprived of their liberty without recourse to the courts, or sentenced at age 13 to a six-year sentence (care order) for a relatively minor offence. Chapter 2 has shown how in the USA the use of the treatment model and the justification of indeterminate sentences on treatment grounds has eroded the rights of women offenders. The female juvenile belongs to the group of offenders most at risk from the vagaries of the welfare/treatment model. The overrepresentation of females in proceedings arising out of status offences, and the sexualization of female offending, has been discussed earlier. Female juveniles would have much to gain from a separation of the welfare and justice functions of the juvenile courts. Morris et al. (1980) suggest that the juvenile court should deal only with those children who are persistent or serious delinquents and should ensure the safeguarding of legal rights; the principles associated with this justice model would involve seven principles (ibid., pp.68–82).

'The principle of the commission of an offence' would ensure that young people appear in court only for offences which would be punishable if committed by an adult. Status offences would be excluded and females would clearly gain.

'The principle of proportionality of sanctions' would involve a more sophisticated coding of offences by seriousness than the present division into summary and indictable offences, and a coding of dispositions appropriate to the seriousness of the offence charged.

'The principle of determinate sentences' would ensure that committal to care of juveniles would be determined by the court, and since evidence has been reviewed in Chapter 2 that females tend to be institutionalized for longer periods than males, then clearly they would gain from this proposal.

The principles of 'the least restrictive alternative', 'the juvenile's right to counsel', 'of limitations on intervention prior to adjudication' (i.e. limitations on remand) and 'of visibility and accountability in decision-making' would improve justice for both male and female juvenile offenders.

Whilst the notion of a return to a justice approach for juveniles with welfare functions being separate and independent has attractions in attempting to deal with the injustices experienced by female juveniles, there are nevertheless political implications and dangers. The welfare approach 'is attacked on all sides: by conservatives, because it insufficiently encompasses punishment and social control; by liberals, because the legal rights of the individual are threatened; and by radicals, because it is based on false assumptions about the nature of delinquency, paying too little attention to causes to be found in the social structure' (Elliott, 1981, p.67). We have now witnessed the growth of a new and powerful political right in Britain and there is a danger that a move to a justice approach would be supported by it for the wrong reasons. Any move to a justice system would need to be supported by an emphasis on legal rights and by the adequate maintenance of the welfare services. There is no evidence, from this study, that a welfare approach is more justified for girls than for boys when the social backgrounds of the male and female sample were compared and the move to separate welfare and justice functions in working with young offenders would be a welcome innovation.

Diversion is another aspect of social policy raised by the findings of the present study. It might be more accurate to record lack of diversion, since although it is evident from the data that many of the young people in the present study were young (10—13 years), first-time petty offenders, nevertheless at the consultative panel stage no case received a recommendation of 'No further action' — an option open to the panels. The part played by the system itself in the development of criminal careers needs to be set alongside the knowledge that most young people 'grow out' of their delinquency by the time they reach their early twenties. The use of the cumbersome, expensive and stigmatizing process of the juvenile court for petty offences loses its effectiveness for the more serious and persistent offender. In Britain the issue of diversion has not been seriously addressed, but it would seem that the consultative panels could have an important part to play in bringing about effective diversion of some youngsters from the system. Sarri's (1983) summary of evaluations of the effectiveness diversion programmes in the USA, whilst cautionary, offers a convincing and positive alternative approach to dealing with some young offenders. In the police consultative panels the germ of a diversion system is already in operation. What is needed is a change in political will to make that aspect of the panels' work operative.

Unemployment and juvenile justice

An interesting and disturbing (but not unexpected) aspect to the data on the social background of the young offenders concerns the employment status of the young people (see Table 5.22) and of their fathers (see Table 5.24): 44 per cent of the male juveniles not of school age were unemployed, and 72 per cent of the female sample not of school age were unemployed. With regard to the employment status of their fathers, there was no significant difference between the male and female group, but overall 54 per cent of fathers were unemployed. Bearing in mind that the local figures for unemployment at the time of the research were 11.6 per cent in the city and 12.1 per cent in the town, with 9.8 per cent being the national average, then clearly these high percentages of unemployment of the young people themselves, particularly the girls, and of the fathers is a matter of concern. Against this background the medical model as a response to juvenile delinquency seems particularly inept when the young people in the sample are clearly disadvantaged in terms of employment opportunity to this extent. Asquith summarizes the implications so aptly:

> Providing justice for children will not be possible without analysing the way in which life opportunities and experiences are socially distributed. This is essentially a *political* exercise.
> Policies which ignore the economic realities in which children find themselves, while promoting greater equality and justice within formal systems of control, may not only ignore but may compound the structural and material inequalities which have historically been associated with criminal behaviour. The provision of justice for children will require a fundamental reappraisal of life opportunities offered to children. (Asquith, 1983, p.17)

Sarri (1983, p.71) also emphasizes the importance of improving opportunities: 'Clearly, increases in legitimate opportunities for youth must be pursued with far greater resources and effort than has been exhibited in the present or past decade.' This lack of attention to economic and structural issues in understanding, explaining and responding to delinquency is paralleled by a similar neglect in the analysis of female crime. A number of recent commentators (e.g. Weis, 1976; Smart, 1976; Campbell, 1981; Box, 1983) have emphasized economic pressures and their impact on female crime, yet neither those fully committed to the Women's movement nor the Radical Criminologists have yet addressed the issue seriously in relation to female crime. It is of course a factor affecting both male and female crime, and thus underlines the fact that research into female crime should guard against separatism. In the end, the causes of male and female crime may be more similar than has been hitherto accepted.

Professional education for social welfare roles

> The overriding problem with much of the existing work on the discretion of the police and courts in their treatment of offenders is that it presumes the existence of an attitude of benevolence and chivalry on the part of law enforcement agencies towards female offenders. Previous studies have failed to distinguish between the types or categories of offences and have relied too heavily on incomplete and unreliable statistical sources with the result that the initial pre-suppositions receive confirmation and the complexity of the situation remains unrecognised. A critical approach to the often stated and implied belief in the favourable treatment of women by the agents of law enforcement is therefore scientifically necessary; certainly until further studies are completed, such beliefs should be viewed with scepticism. (Smart, 1976, p.139)

The above paragraph has been quoted at length because it summarizes the intention and the core of the present research. It has made, it is hoped, a contribution to the call for research on the existence of gender bias in the juvenile process at least, and certainly the results do show clearly the complexity anticipated by Smart.

The fact that none of the research hypotheses of the present study, deliberately formulated to reflect the common view of the courts' dealings with females, was fully upheld by the results highlights, as has been suggested, the need for professionals to review their attitudes and decision-making with regard to female offenders. In discussing procedures for setting up data collection for the present study with a police inspector (female), the researcher was received with some amusement: the reason for this became apparent on being told that there was no need to set up a research project with all the work entailed, for it was clear to anyone who had dealings with the juvenile courts and the consultative panels, that female juveniles were treated more leniently than males. It was fortunate that the research had already received approval from a higher rank and so was facilitated.

The complexity and differential occurrence of gender bias evident from the research reported here, as well as the evidence from the literature review, suggests that there is room for further research in this field. The present study did not include an evaluation of the attitudes of court officials, police officers, magistrates and social workers, but this aspect of gender bias could well throw further light on its complex pattern of incidence. There is evidence from the present study to shake the myth of chivalry in the juvenile justice system, but it will take time and more research to dig it out from its well-established roots.

One way of changing attitudes is through education. Basic qualifying courses and post-qualifying courses for social workers have only recently begun to address gender issues such as mental illness, women and social workers. The treatment of female juveniles by the social services, the probation service and the courts is an area needing promotion in professional education.

The attitudes of the social work agencies — social services, probation and education welfare — to the young offenders in the sample is disturbing. There was little sense of these agencies acting as advocates for the young people, or acting as consultants in a professional sense within the panels. Many social services based social workers would acknowledge the difficulty they experience in operating within the conflicting roles of both welfare and justice ideologies. Their professional identity appears to be confused in this area of practice, a conclusion borne out by recent evaluations of Social Inquiry Reports (Harris, 1982; Osborne, 1984; Webb, 1984). It is an issue needing attention at basic qualifying and post-qualifying training levels.

There is, however, a wider issue of the way in which social workers operate in an interdisciplinary context. Social work with the mentally ill, hospital service work, child guidance based social work and residential service work all require interdisciplinary co-operation. Perhaps one of the most testing areas of this is the interdisciplinary case conference which it is now common practice to hold in cases of suspected child abuse in most local authorities. The consultative panels also are clearly a forum where social work values and ideology could be brought to influence the juvenile system, and it is with dismay that the researcher reports the findings in this area. Professional identity in social work is weak. Perhaps one area where its identity is strongest is in clinical social work with its therapeutic image and association with the medical model. Little wonder that social workers faced with implementing social control of young offenders are uncertain of their professional identity and are often regarded as ineffective in either the care or the control role.

Finally, there is a wider issue related to attitudes towards women in our society. Ten years or more of the Women's movement have had some impact, but this has been largely on the middle-class woman. It has left the average working-class woman and girl untouched by its influence, indeed even alienated by some of its more extreme forms. Attitudes to adolescent female offenders involve deeply rooted attitudes towards female sexuality and the female gender role in our society. Perhaps research, such as the present study, can contribute a little by challenging commonly held views, and by doing so, thus help to accelerate the inevitably slow progress to a more enlightened society:

> Correction should forget the image of the fallen woman and instead view her as a woman who needs skills to change the conditions of her life. (Velimesis, 1975, p.111)

> The notion of a 'chivalrous' justice system, so convincingly described by criminologists of the past and present, is only one of many myths concerning the nature of female crime. It is a myth which has been publicised by many writers, but challenged and researched by few. (Anderson, 1976, p.355)

Appendix I: Questionnaire to obtain data on offences charged and previous record

School of Social Work. Research Project on Juvenile Offenders.

1. Case Number................ 2. Age (years/months)........... 3. Sex........

4. Date of this Court Appearance...............................

5. Reasons for this Court Appearance (including *offences charged*, where applicable). Please include value of property offences:

1	
2	
3	
4	
5	
6	
7	
8	

6. Referred by:

Police	
Local Authority	
Other (please specify)	

7. In cases where offences are charged, please indicate associates charged on same offences:

Alone	
With friends (please indicate no.)	
With siblings (please indicate no.)	

8. Plea:

Guilty	
Not guilty	
Not applicable	
Other	

9. Is the Juvenile represented by a Lawyer?

Yes	
No	

10. Dates and details of previous Court Appearances:

	Date of appearance	Charges	Associates	Disposal
1				
2				
3				
4				
5				
6				

11. Dates and details of Police Cautions received by this Juvenile:

	Date of Caution	Charges	Associates
1			
2			
3			
4			

12. Has a Social Inquiry Report been presented to the Court by the following?

SSD	
Probation	
No SERs	

13. Recommendation contained in SER..
....
....
....

14. Other written reports presented to the Court by:

	Recommendations
Psychiatrist	
Psychologist	
EWO	
School	
Medical	
Superintendent, Children's Home	
Other (please specify)	

15. Court disposal at this appearance..
....
....

Appendix II: Questionnaire to obtain data on social background

School of Social Work. Research Project on Juvenile Offenders

1. Case Number..
2. Area of Residence ....
   ....
3. Age...................................... 4. Sex..............................
5. Name of School Attended..
   ....

or

6. a If the young person is employed, please indicate:
   i   length of time in present job (years/months)......................
   ii   nature of duties...
   iii name profession, industry or business................................
   iv   approximate earnings...................................

b If the young person has had jobs previously, please indicate:

Nature of duties	Industry/ business	Length of time	Approximate earnings
1			
2			
3			

c If the young person is at present unemployed, please state for how long:

years   months   weeks

....

d If the young person has been unemployed on previous occasions, please indicate number of occasions and for how long:

Occasions	Length of time unemployed years months weeks

7. Where is the young person's permanent home considered to be?

1	With natural Mother and Father (married)	
2	With natural Mother and Father (cohabiting)	
3	With Mother living alone	
4	With Father living alone	
5	With natural Mother and cohabitee	
6	With natural Mother and Stepfather	
7	With natural Father and cohabitee	
8	With natural Father and Stepmother	
9	With other relative or guardian (specify please)	
10	With persons unrelated to juvenile and not legal guardian (specify please)	
11	Other (specify please)	

8. Parents' Ages:

	years
Mother	
Father	

9. Parents' Employment:

	Nature of duties	Industry, profession or business	If part time, please state no. of hours	Length of time employed	Approximate earnings
Mother					
Father					

10. If either parent is unemployed, please state for how long:

Mother	
Father	

11. If either parent has been in present job for less than 12 months, please give the following information about previous job:

	Nature of duties	Industry, profession or business	If part time, please state no. of hours	Length of time employed	Approximate earnings
Mother					
Father					

12. Is either parent receiving supplementary benefit?

	Yes/No	How long?
Mother		
Father		

13. Has either parent served one or more prison sentence?

	Yes/No	No. of sentences	Length of sentence	Offence
Mother				
Father				

14. Has either parent been found guilty of offences charged by a court of law, and resulting in a sentence other than prison?

	Offence charged	Sentence
Mother		
Father		

15. Has the young person been in substitute care?

	No. of occasions	Length of time
With a relative		
In Foster Care		
In a Children's Home		
In an Assessment Centre		
In a CHE		
Other (please specify)		

16. Housing

Is the parental home: No. of rooms:

Rented (council)			Living	
Rented (private)			Bedrooms	
Owner occupied			Kitchen	
Owner occupied (mortgaged)			Bathroom	
Other (please specify)			Garden	
			Garage	

17. Is the parental home:

Terraced		Detached	
Semi-detached		Mobile Home	
Other (please specify)			

18. Siblings of the Juvenile:

Name	Age (years)	Sex (M/F)	Known to Probation/SSD (Yes/No)	Has appeared in Court, (Yes/No)	No. of occasions	Reasons	Sentence(s)
1							
2							
3							
4							

Please indicate below siblings not living at home and reason(s):

Appendix III: Questionnaire to obtain data on the consultative panels

School of Social Work. Research Project on Juvenile Offenders.

Please enter details of each juvenile considered by the Consultative Panel.

1. Case No............... 2. Age (years/months).................... 3. Sex.......
4. History of Offending

    a Previous Court Appearances (where applicable):

	Date	Offences charged	Court disposal	Date
1				
2				
3				
4				
5				

b Previous considerations by Consultative Panel (where applicable):

	Date	Offences	Panel recommendation	Superintendent's decision
1				
2				
3				
4				

5. Details of Current Offence(s):

	Offence	Date
1		
2		
3		
4		
5		
6		

6. Date of Panel Meeting..

7. Agency Recommendations in Consultative Panel Meeting:

Agency	Recommendation
Police	
Probation	
Social Services	
Education Welfare	

8. Panel Recommendation to Superintendent...................................

9. Superintendent's Decision..

(June 1981)

Bibliography

Adler, F. (1975), *Sisters in Crime: The Rise of the New Female Criminal*, New York, McGraw-Hill.

Adler, F. and Simon, R.J. (eds) (1979), *The Criminology of Deviant Women*, Boston, Mass., Houghton Mifflin.

Ainsworth, M.D. (1962), 'The effects of maternal deprivation', in Ainsworth, M.D. (ed.), *Deprivation of Maternal Care: A Reassessment of its Effects*, Geneva, World Health Organization.

Akers, R.L. (1964), 'Socio-economic status and delinquent behaviour: a re-test', *Journal of Research in Crime and Delinquency*, 1, pp.38–46.

Anderson, E.A. (1976), 'The "chivalrous" treatment of the female offender in the arms of the criminal justice system: a review of the literature', *Social Problems*, 23, pp.350–7.

Andrew, J.M. (1976), 'Delinquency, sex and family variables', *Social Biology*, 23, 2, pp.168–71.

Andry, R.G. (1960), *Delinquency and Parental Pathology: A Study in Clinical and Forensic Psychology*, London, Methuen.

Armstrong, G. (1977), 'Females under the law — "protected" but unequal', *Crime and Delinquency*, 23, 2, pp.109–20.

Asquith, S. (1983), 'Justice, retribution and children', in Morris, A. and Giller, H. (eds), *Providing Criminal Justice for Children*, London, Edward Arnold, ch.1.

Balch, R.W. (1975), 'The medical model of delinquency', *Crime and Delinquency*, 21, 2, pp.116–30.

Bandura, A. and Walters, R.H. (1958), 'Dependency conflicts in aggressive delinquents', *Journal of Social Issues*, 14, pp.52–65.

Barker, G. and Adams, W. (1962), 'Comparisons of the delinquencies of boys and girls', *Journal of Criminal Law, Criminology and Police Science*, 53, pp.470–5.

Becker, H.S. (1963), *Outsiders: Studies in the Sociology of Deviance*, New York, The Free Press.

Bennett, I. (1960), *Delinquent and Neurotic Children*, New York, Basic Books.

Blos, P. (1969), 'Three typical constellations of female delinquency', in Pollok, O. and Friedman, A.S. (eds), *Family Dynamics and Female Sexual Delinquency*, Palo Alto, Calif., Science and Behaviour Books, ch.10.

Bowker, L.H. *et al.* (eds) (1978), *Women, Crime and the Criminal Justice System*, Lexington, Mass., Lexington Books.

Bowlby, J. (1947), *Forty-four Juvenile Thieves: Their Characters and Home Life*, London, Baillière, Tindall & Cox.

Bowlby, J. (1951), *Maternal Care and Mental Health*, Geneva, World Health Organization.

Box, S. (1983), *Power, Crime and Mystification*, London, Tavistock.

Burt, C. (1925), *The Young Delinquent*, New York, D. Appleton.

Bushong, E. (1926), 'Family estrangement and juvenile delinquency', *Social Forces*, 5, pp.79–83.

Campbell, A. (1976), The role of the peer group in female delinquency', D.Phil. thesis, University of Oxford.

Campbell, A. (1981), *Girl Delinquents*, Oxford, Basil Blackwell.

Caplan, P.J. *et al.* (1980), 'Sex differences in a delinquent clinic population', *British Journal of Criminology*, 20, 4, pp.311–28.

Casburn, M. (1979), *Girls Will Be Girls: Sexism and Juvenile Justice in a London Borough*, Explorations in Feminism No.6, London, Women's Research and Resources Centre.

Cernkovich, S.A. and Giordano, P. (1979), 'A comparative analysis of male and female delinquency', *Sociological Quarterly*, 20, 1, pp.131 –45.

Chapman, J.R. (1980), *Economic Realities and the Female Offender*, Lexington, Mass., D.C. Heath.

Chesney-Lind, M. (1973), 'Judicial enforcement of the female sex-role: the family court and the female delinquent', *Issues in Criminology*, 8, 2, pp.51–69.

Chesney-Lind, M. (1974), 'Juvenile delinquency: the sexualisation of female crime', *Psychology Today*, 8, pp.43–6.

Chesney-Lind, M. (1977), 'Judicial paternalism and the female status offender: training women to know their place', *Crime and Delinquency*, 23, pp.121–30.

Chesney-Lind, M. (1978), 'Young women in the arms of the law', in Bowker, L.H. *et al.* (eds), *Women, Crime and the Criminal Justice System*, Lexington, Mass., Lexington Books, ch.6.

Cicourel, A. (1968), *The Social Organisation of Juvenile Justice*, London, Heinemann.

Clark, J.P. and Haurek, E. (1966), 'Age and sex roles of adolescents and their involvement in misconduct: a re-appraisal', *Sociology and Social Research*, 50, pp.496–508.

Clark, J.P. and Taft, L.L. (1966), 'Polygraph and interview validation of self-reported deviant behaviour among juveniles', *American Sociological Review*, 27, pp.826–34.

Clark, J.P. and Wenninger (1962), 'Socio-economic class and area as correlates of illegal behaviour among juveniles', *American Sociological Review*, 27, pp.826–34.

Clark, S.M. (1967), 'Systematic comparison of female and male delinquency', in Reckless, W.C. (ed.), *The Crime Problem*, New York, Appleton-Century-Crofts.

Clements, C. (1972), 'Sex and sentencing', *South Western Law Journal*, 26, pp.890–904.

Cloward, R.A. and Ohlin, L.E. (1960), *Delinquency and Opportunity*, London, Routledge & Kegan Paul.

Cockburn, J.J. and Maclay, I. (1965), 'Sex differentials in juvenile delinquency', *British Journal of Criminology*, 5, pp.289–308.

Cohen, A. (1955), *Delinquent Boys: The Culture of the Gang*, New York, The Free Press.

Cohen, L.E. (1975), *Juvenile Dispositions: Social and Legal Factors Related to the Processing of Denver Delinquency Cases*, Washington, DC, US Department of Justice.

Cohn, Y. (1963), 'Criteria for the probation officer's recommendation to the juvenile court judge', *Crime and Delinquency*, 9, pp.262–75.

Conway, A. and Bogodan, C. (1977), 'Sexual delinquency. The persistence of a double standard', *Crime and Delinquency*, 23, pp.130–5.

Cowie, J., Cowie, V. and Slater, E. (1968), *Delinquency in Girls*, London, Heinemann.

Crites, L. (ed.) (1976), *The Female Offender*, Lexington, Mass., D.C. Heath.

Datesman, S.K. and Scarpitti, F. (1980), 'Unequal protection for males and females in the juvenile court', in Datesman, S.K. and Scarpitti, F. (eds), *Women, Crime and Justice*, New York, Oxford University Press.

Datesman, S.K. and Scarpitti, F. (eds) (1980), *Women, Crime and Justice*, New York, Oxford University Press.

Datesman, S.K., Scarpitti, F. and Stephenson, R.M. (1975), 'Female delinquency: an application of self and opportunity theories', *Journal of Research in Crime and Delinquency*, 12, pp.107–23.

Davies, J. (1976), *Girls Appearing before a Juvenile Court*, London, HMSO.

Dentler, R.A. and Monroe, L.J. (1961), 'Social correlates of early adolescent theft', *American Sociological Review*, 26, pp.733–43.

DHSS (1981), *Offending by Young People: A Survey of Recent Trends*, London, DHSS.

Ditchfield, J.A. (1976), *Police Cautioning in England and Wales*, Home Office Research Study 37, London, HMSO.

Downes, D. (1966), *The Delinquent Solution: A Study of Subcultural Theory*, London, Routledge & Kegan Paul.

Elliott, D. (1981), 'Juvenile justice', in Jones, H. (ed.), *Society Against Crime*, Harmondsworth, Penguin, ch.2.

Farrington, D.P. (1973), 'Self reports of deviant behaviour: predictive and stable?', *Journal of Criminal Law and Criminology*, 64, pp.99–110.

FBI (1980), *Uniform Crime Reports: Crime in the United States 1979*, Washington, DC, US Department of Justice.

Felice, M. and Offord, D. (1971), 'Girl delinquency', *Corrective Psychiatry and Journal of Social Therapy*, 17, 2, pp.18–33.

Felice, M. and Offord, D. (1972), 'Three developmental pathways to delinquency in girls', *British Journal of Criminology*, 12, pp.375–89.

Feyerhem, W. (1981), 'Measuring gender differences in delinquency self-reports versus police contact', in Warren, M. (ed.), *Comparing Female and Male Offenders*, Beverly Hills, Calif. and London, Sage, ch.3.

Fielding, J. (1977), 'Juvenile delinquency', in Wilson, P.R. (ed.), *Delinquency in Australia*, St Lucia, Queensland, University of Queensland Press, ch.8.

Figueira-McDonough, J. *et al.* (1981), 'Normal deviance. Gender similarities in adolescent subcultures', in Warren, M.Q. (ed.), *Comparing Female and Male Offenders*, Beverly Hills, Calif. and London, Sage, ch.2.

Friedman, A.S. (1969), 'The family and the female delinquent: an overview', in Pollok, O. and Friedman, A.S. (eds), *Family Dynamics and Female Sexual Delinquency*, Palo Alto, Calif., Science and Behaviour Books.

Gelsthorpe, L. (1981), *Girls in the Juvenile Court: Defining the Terrain of Penal Policy*, London, Justice for Children.

Gibbons, D. and Griswold, M. (1957), 'Sex differences among juvenile court referrals', *Sociology and Social Research*, 5, 42, pp.106–10.

Gibbons, H.B., Morrison, J. and West, J. (1970), 'The confessions of known offenders in response to a self-reported delinquency schedule', *British Journal of Criminology*, 22, pp.51–65.

Gilbert, J. (1972), 'Delinquent (approved school) and non-delinquent (secondary modern school) girls', *British Journal of Criminology*, 12, pp.325—56.

Glueck, S. and Glueck, E. (1934), *Five Hundred Delinquent Women*, New York, Knopf.

Glueck, S. and Glueck, E. (1952), *Delinquents in the Making: Paths to Prevention*, New York, Harper & Row.

Gold, M. (1970), *Delinquent Behaviour in an American City*, Belmont, Calif., Brooks Cole.

Gold, S. (1971), 'Equal protection for juvenile girls in need of supervision in New York state', *New York Law Forum*, 17, p.593.

Gold, M. and Reimer, D.J. (1975), 'Changing patterns of delinquent behaviour among Americans 13 through 16 years old, 1967—1972', *Crime and Delinquency Literature*, 7, pp.483—517.

Goldman, N. (1963), *The Differential Selection of Juvenile Offenders for Court Appearance*, National Council on Crime and Delinquency.

Gordon, D. (1973), 'Captialism, class and crime in America', *Crime and Delinquency*, 19, pp.163—84.

Grichting, W.L. (1977), 'On the state and fate of status offenders', *Australian and New Zealand Journal of Criminology*, 10, 3, pp.133—51.

Grygier, T. *et al.* (1969), 'Paternal deprivation: a study of delinquent children', *British Journal of Criminology*, 9, 3, pp.209—53.

Hardt, R.H. and Peterson-Hardt, S. (1977), 'On determining the quality of the delinquency self-report method', *Journal of Research in Crime and Delinquency*, 14, pp.247—61.

Harris, R. (1982), 'Institutionalised ambivalence: social work and the Children and Young Persons Act 1969', *British Journal of Social Work*, 12, 3, pp.247—64.

Heidensohn, F. (1968), 'The deviance of women: a critique and an enquiry', *British Journal of Sociology*, 19, pp.160—75.

Hiller, A.E. and Hancock, L. (1981), 'The processing of female juveniles in Victoria', in Mukherjee, S.K. and Scott, J.A. (eds), *Women and Crime*, London, Allen & Unwin/Australian Institute of Criminology.

Hindelang, M. (1969), 'Equality under the law', *Journal of Criminal Law and Criminology*, 60, pp.306—13.

Hindelang, M. (1971a), 'Age, sex and the versatility of delinquent involvements', *Social Problems*, 18, pp.522—34.

Hindelang, M. (1971b), 'The social versus solitary nature of delinquent involvements', *British Journal of Criminology*, 11, pp.167—75.

Hindelang, M. (1976), 'With a little help from their friends: group participation in reported delinquent behaviour', *British Journal of Criminology*, 16, 2, pp.109—25.

Hirschi, J. (1969), *Causes of Delinquency*, Berkeley and Los Angeles, Calif., University of California Press.

Hoffman Bustamante, D. (1973), 'The nature of female criminality', *Issues in Criminology*, 8, 2, pp.117—37.

Home Office (1983), *Criminal Statistics (England and Wales) 1983*, Cmnd 9349, London, HMSO.

Hood, R. and Sparks, R. (1970), *Key Issues in Criminology*, London, Weidenfeld & Nicolson.

Hudson, C.H. (1973), *An Experimental Study of the Differential Effects of Parole Supervision for a Group of Adolescent Boys and Girls: Survey Report*, Washington, DC, US Government Printing Office/US National Institution of Law Enforcement and Criminal Justice.

Jamison, R.N. (1977), 'Personality, anti-social behaviour and risk perception in adolescents', paper delivered at British Psychological Society, London; quoted in Campbell, 1981.

Janes, J.A. (1958), 'The father's part in the development of personality', *Child Welfare*, 37, pp.12—15.

Jensen, G. and Eve, R. (1976), 'Sex differences in delinquency: an examination of popular sociological explanations', *Criminology*, 13, pp.427—48.

Johnson, R.E. (1979), *Juvenile Delinquency and its Origins*, Cambridge, Cambridge University Press.

Jones, H. (1981), *Society against Crime*, Harmondsworth, Penguin.

Kashani, J.H. *et al*. (1980), 'Patterns of delinquency in boys and girls', *Journal of the American Academy of Child Psychiatry*, 19, pp.300—10.

Kitsuse, J.I. (1962), 'Societal reactions to deviant behaviour: problems of theory and method', *Social Problems*, 9, pp.247—56.

Klein, D. (1973), 'The etiology of female criminality', *Issues in Criminology*, 8, pp.3—30.

Klein, D. and Kress, J. (1976), 'Any woman's blues: a critical overview of women, crime and the criminal justice system', *Crime and Social Justice*, 6, pp.34—49.

Klein, M.W. (ed.) (1978), *The Juvenile Justice System. Criminal Justice System Annals*, New York, Sage, Vol.V.

Koller, K. (1971), 'Parental deprivation, family background and female delinquency', *British Journal of Psychiatry*, 118, pp.319—27.

Konopka, G. (1966), *The Adolescent Girl in Conflict*, Englewood Cliffs, NJ, Prentice-Hall.

Kratcoski, P.C. (1974), 'Differential treatment of delinquent boys and girls in a juvenile court', *Child Welfare*, 53, 1, pp.16—22.

Kratcoski, P.C. and Kratcoski, J.E. (1975), 'Changing patterns in the delinquent activities of boys and girls', *Adolescence*, 10, 37, pp.83—91.

Landau, S.F. (1981), 'Juveniles and the police', *British Journal of Criminology*, 21, 1, pp.27—46.

Lang, D.M., Papenfuhs, R. and Walters, J. (1976), 'Females' perceptions of their fathers', *Family Co-ordinator*, 25, 4, pp.475—81.

Leaper, P. (1974), *Children in Need of Care and Protection*, Melbourne, University of Melbourne Department of Criminology.

Lemert, E. (1951), *Social Pathology: A Systematic Approach to the Theory of Sociopathic Behaviour*, New York, McGraw-Hill.

Leonard, E.B. (1982), *Women, Crime and Society. A Critique of Criminology Theory*, New York, Longman.

Little, A. (1965), 'Parental deprivation, separation and crime: a test on adolescent recidivists', *British Journal of Criminology*, 5, pp.419—30.

Lombroso, C. and Ferraro, W. (1895), *The Female Offender*, London, Fisher & Unwin.

Lukianowicz, N. (1971), 'Juvenile offenders. A study of 50 remand home and training school girls in Northern Ireland', *Acta Psychiatra Scandinavica*, 47, 1, pp.1—37.

Lucianowicz, N. (1972), 'Juvenile offenders: a second group of 50 girls from a remand home in Northern Ireland', *Acta Psychiatra Scandinavica*, 48, 4, pp.300—14.

McCord, J., McCord, W. and Thurber, E. (1962), 'Some effects of paternal absence on male children', *Journal of Abnormal Psychology*, 64, pp.361—9.

Mann, C.R. (1977), 'The juvenile female in the judicial process', PhD thesis, University of Illinois.

Mannarino, A.P. and Marsh, M.E. (1978), 'The relationship between sex-role identification and juvenile delinquency in adolescent girls', *Adolescence*, XII, 52, pp.643—52.

Matza, D. (1964), *Delinquency and Drift*, New York, Wiley.

Mawby, R.I. (1980), 'Sex and crime: the results of a self-report study', *British Journal of Sociology*, 31, pp.525—43.

May, D. (1971), 'Delinquency control and the treatment model: some implications of recent legislation', *British Journal of Criminology*, 11, 4, p.359.

May, D. (1977), 'Delinquent girls before the courts', *Medical Science and Law*, 17, 3, pp.203—12.

Merton, R.K. (1938), 'Social structure and anomie', *American Sociological Review*, 3, pp.672—82.

Miller, P.Y. (n.d.), 'Delinquency and gender', paper at Institute for Juvenile Research; quoted in Datesman and Scarpitti, 1980.

Miller, W. (1958), 'Lower class culture as a generating milieu of gang delinquence', *Journal of Social Issues*, 14, pp.5—19.

Monahan, T.P. (1957a), 'Family status and the delinquent child: a reappraisal and some new findings', *Social Forces*, 35, pp.250—8.

Monahan, T.P. (1957b), 'The trend in broken homes among delinquent children', *Marriage and Family Living*, 19, pp.362–5.

Monahan, T.P. (1970), 'Police dispositions of juvenile offenders: the problem of management and a study of Philadelphia data', *Phylon*, XXI, pp.138–9.

Morris, A. and Giller, H. (eds) (1983), *Providing Criminal Justice for Children*, London, Edward Arnold.

Morris, A. *et al.* (1980), *Justice for Children*, London, Macmillan.

Morris, R. (1964), 'Female delinquency and relational problems', *Social Forces*, 43, pp.82–9.

Mukherjee, S.K. and Scott, J.A. (eds) (1981), *Women and Crime*, London, Allen & Unwin/Australian Institute of Criminology.

Nagel, I.H. and Hagan, J. (1983), *Gender and Crime. Offence Patterns and Criminal Court Sanctions*, Crime and Justice No.4, Chicago, University of Chicago Press.

Nettler, G. (1978), *Explaining Crime*, New York, McGraw-Hill.

Nye, F.I. (1958), *Family Relations and Delinquent Behaviour*, New York, Wiley.

Nye, F.E., Short, J.F. and Olson, V.J. (1958), 'Socio-economic status and delinquent behaviour', *American Journal of Sociology*, 63, 4, pp.381–9.

Oakley, A. (1972), *Sex, Gender and Society*, New York, Harper & Row.

Offord, D.R. *et al.* (1979), 'Broken homes, parental psychiatric illness and female delinquency', *American Journal of Orthopsychiatry*, 49, 2, pp.252–64.

O'Kelly, E. (1965), 'Some observations on the relationships between delinquent girls and their parents', *British Journal of Medical Psychology*, 28, pp.59–66.

Osborne, S. (1984), 'Social inquiry reports in one juvenile court', *British Journal of Social Work*, 14, 4, pp.361–78.

Parker, H. *et al.* (1981), *Receiving Juvenile Justice*, Oxford, Basil Blackwell.

Platt, A. (1969), *The Child Savers*, Chicago, University of Chicago Press.

Pollak, J. (1978), 'Early theories of female criminality', in Bowker, L.H. *et al.* (eds), *Women, Crime and the Criminal Justice System*, Lexington, Mass., Lexington Books, ch.2.

Pollok, O. (1961), *The Criminality of Women*, New York, Barnes.

Pollok, O. and Friedman, A.S. (eds) (1969), *Family Dynamics and Female Sexual Delinquency*, Palo Alto, Calif., Science and Behaviour Books.

Priestley, P., Fears, D. and Fuller, F. (1977), *Justice for Juveniles: The 1969 Children and Young Persons Act. A Case for Reform?*, London, Routledge & Kegan Paul.

Quinney, R. (1973), *Critique of Legal Order: Crime Control in a Capitalist Society*, Boston, Mass., Little, Brown.

Reckless, W.C. (ed.) (1967), *The Crime Problem*, New York, Appleton-Century-Crofts.

Richardson, H. (1969), *Adolescent Girls in Approved Schools*, London, Routledge & Kegan Paul.

Riege, M.G. (1972), 'Parental affection and juvenile delinquency in girls', *British Journal of Criminology*, 12, pp.55—73.

Rutter, M. (1972), *Maternal Deprivation Re-assessed*, Harmondsworth, Penguin.

Rutter, M. and Giller, H. (1983), *Juvenile Delinquency: Trends and Perspectives*, Harmondsworth, Penguin.

Sarri, R.C. (1974), *Under Lock and Key: Juveniles in Jails and Detention*, Ann Arbor, Mich., University of Michigan Press.

Sarri, R.C. (1976), 'Juvenile law: how it penalises females', in Crites, L. (ed.), *The Female Offender*, Lexington, Mass., D.C. Heath.

Sarri, R.C. (1983), 'Paradigms and pitfalls in juvenile justice diversion', in Morris, A. and Giller, H. (eds), *Providing Criminal Justice for Children*, London, Edward Arnold, ch.4.

Sarri, R.C. and Vinter, R.D. (1978), 'Justice for whom? Varieties of juvenile correctional approaches', in Klein, M.W. (ed.), *The Juvenile Justice System*, New York, Sage, ch.7.

Schideler, E.H. (1918), 'Family disintegration and the delinquent boy in the United States', *Journal of Criminal Law and Criminology*, 8, pp.709—32.

Schur, E. (1971), *Labelling Deviant Behaviour: Its Sociological Implications*, New York, Harper & Row.

Shacklady-Smith, L. (1978), 'Sexist assumptions and female delinquency — an empirical investigation', in Smart, C. and Smart, B. (eds), *Women, Sexuality and Control*, London, Routledge & Kegan Paul, ch.6.

Short, J. and Nye, I. (1958), 'Extent of unrecorded juvenile delinquency', *Journal of Criminal Law, Criminology and Police Science*, 49, pp.296—302.

Shover, N. and Norland, S. (1978), 'Sex roles and criminality: science or conventional wisdom?', *Sex Roles*, 4, 1, pp.111—25.

Simon, R.J. (1975), *Women and Crime*, Lexington, Mass., Lexington Books.

Simon, R.J. and Sharma, N. (1979), 'Women and crime: does the American experience generalise?', in Adler, F. and Simon, R.J. (eds), *The Criminology of Deviant Women*, Boston, Mass., Houghton Mifflin.

Slawson, J. (1923), 'Marital relations of parents and juvenile delinquency', *Journal of Delinquency*, 8, pp.280—3.

Smart, C. (1976), *Women, Crime and Criminology: A Feminist Critique*, London, Routledge & Kegan Paul.

Smart, C. (1977), 'Criminology theory: its ideology and implications concerning women', *British Journal of Sociology*, 28, pp.89–100.

Smart, C. (1979), 'The New Female Criminal: reality or myth?', *British Journal of Criminology*, 19, 1, pp.50–9.

Smart, C. and Smart, B. (eds) (1978), *Women, Sexuality and Control*, London, Routledge & Kegan Paul.

Smith, D.A. and Visher, A.C. (1980), 'Sex and involvement in deviance/crime. A quantitative review of the empirical literature', *American Sociological Review*, 45, pp.691–701.

Spitzer, S. (1975), 'Towards a Marxist theory of deviance', *Social Problems*, 2, pp.638–51.

Steer, D. (1970), *Police Cautions – a Study in the Exercise of Police Discretion*, Oxford, Oxford University Penal Research Unit/Basil Blackwell.

Steffensmeir, D. (1980), 'Sex differences in patterns of adult crimes 1965–77. A review and assessment', *Social Forces*, 58, pp.1080–1108.

Sutherland, E.H. and Cressey, D.R. (1960), *Principles of Criminology*, New York, Lippincott (first published 1924).

Tappan, P. (1947), *Delinquent Girls in Court*, New York, Columbia University Press.

Taylor, I., Walton, P. and Young, J. (1973), *The New Criminology. For a Social Theory of Deviance*, New York, Harper & Row.

Taylor, I., Walton, P. and Young, J. (1975), *Critical Criminology*, London, Routledge & Kegan Paul.

Teilmann, K.S. and Landry, P.H., Jr (1981), 'Gender bias in juvenile justice', *Journal of Research in Crime and Delinquency*, 18, pp.47–80.

Terry, R.M. (1967), 'Discrimination in the handling of juvenile offenders by social control agencies', *Journal of Research in Crime and Delinquency*, 4, pp.218–30.

Thomas, W.I. (1923), *The Unadjusted Girl*, New York, Harper & Row.

Thorpe, D.H. *et al.* (1980), *Out of Care: The Community Support of Juvenile Offenders*, London, Allen & Unwin.

Trèse, L.J. (1962), *101 Delinquent Girls*, Notre Dame, Ind., Fides.

Vaz, E. (ed.) (1967), *Middle Class Juvenile Delinquency*, New York, Harper & Row.

Vedder, C.B. and Somerville, D.B. (1970), *The Delinquent Girl*, Springfield, Ill., Charles C. Thomas.

Velimesis, M. (1975), 'The female offender', *Crime and Delinquency Literature*, pp.94–112.

Voss, H.L. (1966), 'Socio-economic status and reported delinquent behaviour', *Social Problems*, 13, pp.314—24.

Walberg, H.J. and Yeh, E.G. (1974), 'Family background, ethnicity and urban delinquency', *Journal of Research in Crime and Delinquency*, 11, pp.80—7.

Warren, M.Q. (ed.) (1981), *Comparing Female and Male Offenders*, Research Progress in Criminology No.21, Beverly Hills, Calif. and London, Sage.

Wattenberg, W. and Saunders, F. (1954), 'Sex differences among juvenile offenders', *Sociology and Social Research*, 38, pp.24—31.

Wattenberg, W.W. and Saunders, F. (1955), 'Recidivism among girls', *Journal of Abnormal and Social Psychology*, 50, pp.405—6.

Webb, D. (1984), 'Girl offenders on supervision', *Sociology*, 18, 3, pp.367—81.

Weeks, H. (1940), 'Male and female broken home rates by types of delinquency', *American Sociological Review*, 5, pp.601—9.

Weis, J. (1975), 'Middle class female delinquency', paper presented at Annual Meeting of American Society of Criminology, Toronto; reported in Datesman and Scarpitti, 1981.

Weis, J. (1976), 'Liberation and crime: the invention of the new female criminal', *Crime and Social Justice*, 6, pp.17—27.

West, D. and Farrington, D.R. (1973), *Who Becomes Delinquent?*, London, Heinemann.

Williams, J.R. and Gold, M. (1972), 'From delinquent behaviour to official delinquency', *Social Problems*, 20, pp.209—29.

Wilson, H. (1975), 'Juvenile delinquency, parental criminality and social handicap', *British Journal of Criminology*, 15, 3, pp.241—50.

Wise, N. (1967), 'Juvenile delinquency among middle class girls', in Vaz, E. (ed.), *Middle Class Juvenile Delinquency*, New York, Harper & Row.

Yablonsky, L. (1962), *The Violent Gang*, New York, Macmillan.

Index

Research design 14, 52—60
Research methodology 14, 36
Runaways 27, 29, 30, 38, 45

Sampling 13, 52—6
School attendance 33
Self-report studies 3, 13—23, 24, 26, 30, 38, 64
Sentencing 37, 42
Sex differences 26
Sex offences 18, 24, 29, 32
Sex-role 9, 10, 23, 33, 39
Sexual activities 27
Sexual behaviour 25, 29
Sexual delinquency 7, 20, 24
Sexual deviancy 8
Sexual history 6, 29
Sexual taboos 25
Sexualization of female crime 5, 8, 26, 38, 117
Shoplifting 32, 64, 85, 96
Siblings 51
Social class 23, 44, 48, 51, 107
Social background 42—4, 50
Social disadvantage 33
Social inquiry reports 35, 51, 104, 121
Social services 53, 54, 57—60, 76—8, 83—5, 105, 109, 112, 113, 121
Social worker 80, 103
Socio-economic factors 45, 118—19

Socio-economic status 26, 48—9, 54, 88, 106—8, 112, 114
SPSS 30, 57
Status offences 18, 19, 20, 21, 24, 25, 26, 29, 30, 32, 33, 34, 35, 38, 40, 41, 45, 118
Sub-cultural theory 2, 4
Substitute care 51, 101—3, 113, 114
Supervision 29, 32, 33, 35, 36, 40, 89, 96
Supplementary benefit 108

Teenage culture 21
Theft 24, 31, 32
Training school 27, 38, 45
Treatment model *see* Medical model
Truancy 28, 41

Unemployment 52—3, 106—8, 113, 119—20

Welfare model 25, 40, 41, 42, 80, 100, 105, 112, 117
Welfare services 24
Women's liberation 11
Women's movement 10, 11, 12, 120, 122
Women's role 5, 10, 11, 65, 81
Working class 4, 17, 22, 108

Youth culture 20